# me, myself, & lies

## & lies

for young women

JENNIFER ROTHSCHILD

HARVEST HOUSE PUBLISHERS
EUGENE, OREGON

Cover design by Rightly Designed

Cover Image © nikiteev / Adobe Stock Images

**ME, MYSELF, AND LIES FOR YOUNG WOMEN**
Copyright © 2017 Jennifer Rothschild
Published by Harvest House Publishers
Eugene, Oregon 97402
www.harvesthousepublishers.com

ISBN 978-0-7369-6421-0 (pbk.)
ISBN 978-0-7369-6422-7 (eBook)

Names: Rothschild, Jennifer, 1963- author.
Title: Me, myself, and lies for young women / Jennifer Rothschild.
Description: Eugene, Oregon : Harvest House Publishers, 2017.
Identifiers: LCCN 2016033249 (print) | LCCN 2017006993 (ebook) | ISBN 9780736964210 (pbk.) | ISBN 9780736964227 ()
Subjects: LCSH: Teenage girls—Religious life. | Christian teenagers—Religious life. | Teenage girls—Conduct of life. | Christian teenagers—Conduct of life. | Self-talk—Religious aspects—Christianity. | Truthfulness and falsehood—Religious aspects—Christianity.
Classification: LCC BV4551.3 .R68 2017 (print) | LCC BV4551.3 (ebook) | DDC 248.8/33—dc23
LC record available at https://lccn.loc.gov/2016033249

**Printed in the United States of America.**

17  18  19  20  21  22  23  24  25  /  BP-KBD  /  10  9  8  7  6  5  4  3  2  1

# Contents

**Part 1—Talking Truth to Yourself**

1. Go Through Your Closet . . . . . . . . . . . . . . . . . . . . . 9

2. Keep or Toss? . . . . . . . . . . . . . . . . . . . . . . . . . . . 23

3. Perfectly Imperfect . . . . . . . . . . . . . . . . . . . . . . . 39

4. Tune In . . . . . . . . . . . . . . . . . . . . . . . . . . . . . . . 55

**Part 2 —Seven Must-Have Pieces for Your Thought Closet**

5. Piece #1: Daily Maintenance . . . . . . . . . . . . . . . . 73

6. Piece #2: Hope . . . . . . . . . . . . . . . . . . . . . . . . . . 89

7. Piece #3: Water . . . . . . . . . . . . . . . . . . . . . . . . . 105

8. Piece #4: Memory . . . . . . . . . . . . . . . . . . . . . . . 121

9. Piece #5: Chill . . . . . . . . . . . . . . . . . . . . . . . . . . 137

10. Piece #6: Perseverance . . . . . . . . . . . . . . . . . . . . 155

11. Piece #7: Heart . . . . . . . . . . . . . . . . . . . . . . . . . 169

An Invite . . . . . . . . . . . . . . . . . . . . . . . . . . . . . . 181

## Part 1

# TALKING TRUTH TO YOURSELF

Let's get real here—right from the start! Have you ever talked to yourself? Either out loud or just in your mind? (You know, that little voice in your head that whispers questions and doubts and random ideas?) It's okay to go ahead and admit it, because we all talk to ourselves. The thing is, talking to ourselves is so natural that we usually don't even think about it. And because we don't think about it, we don't take time to think about what exactly we're saying to ourselves.

I have a name for this kind of talking to yourself: *soul talk*.

I like to call it this because the soul is that inner part of you that makes you, *you*. It's the deepest part of who you are. It's what makes you unique and special and different from everyone else. Your soul is also what connects you to God.

Soul talk can be a really great thing. But it can also be very negative and damaging if we don't stop to consider whether the things we're telling ourselves are even true. And that's a huge problem because a lot of what we tell ourselves is actually false. Of course we don't set out to tell ourselves lies, but every day we take in tons of messages from the world around us that make us start doubting our own value…and then we lie to ourselves about who we are. And even worse, we believe them.

If we start believing these lies, our lives can get kind of messed up. But if whatever we tell ourselves is real and true—if our soul talk consists of words of truth that line up with what God's Word says—we experience joy and encouragement and hope and peace and a lot of other good things.

Our soul talk is incredibly powerful! Whatever we tell ourselves goes straight to our hearts and our minds. Those words—even if they aren't true—shape the way we think about ourselves. They influence our emotions, our thoughts, and our decisions. They affect our relationships with other people. They can make a big difference in every part of our lives—family, friends, school, activities, church...even our hobbies and interests.

When it comes to your mind and your heart, though, there's no room for lies. You only want truth there! And that's what we're going to discover together—some awesome ways to make sure the words you're telling yourself are words of truth that God Himself would also say to you.

Things like...

> *You matter.*
> *You are special.*
> *You're the beautiful girl God created!*

You know, the truth!

# 1

# GO THROUGH YOUR CLOSET

Haley pulled her favorite purple T-shirt over her head and slipped into a well-worn pair of jeans. But when she looked in the mirror, she noticed that the shirt had a toothpaste stain right in the front, and the jeans...Well, most girls weren't wearing that style anymore—but they were so comfortable!

She was going to be late for school if she didn't change quickly, but Haley couldn't find anything in her closet she wanted to wear. The last time she'd worn a dress, a few kids had made fun of her—even though it was a simple T-shirt dress—and told her she looked too dressed up. Her other shirts seemed too bright and colorful. Neutrals were the thing now at her school. And she couldn't find another clean pair of jeans.

*All my stuff is wrong*, Haley thought.
*And nothing looks good on me anyway.*
*How could it? I'm just not as pretty as the other girls.*
*Come to think of it, I'm not as smart either.*
*Or as talented. Or as popular.*
*I'll never measure up!*

• • •

Have you ever had a getting-ready-for-school morning like Haley's? Have you ever stood in front of a mirror and told yourself all the specific ways you don't measure up? And then maybe you picked up your phone and started scrolling through Instagram or Tumblr and started comparing yourself—your unfiltered, no-makeup, dirty T-shirt self—to the seemingly perfect images captured on camera (which, by the way, are filtered and fully edited pictures of women who are completely made up). Those pictures can make us crazy with the standards they set for us.

And that can happen even when you're just talking to the self you see in the mirror. This craziness gets even worse when you throw in the things other people are saying about you—or the things you *think* they might be saying! Believe me, sometimes—a lot of the time—we misread a situation. We see someone whispering to someone else, and when they glance our way we think, *It's obvious they're talking about me.* Or we read something online and guess, *This is totally referring to me.*

Guess what? More untruths.

Yep. More lies.

More stuff we need to clean out of our thought closets.

Because you know what the truth really is? You *do* measure up. You *are* talented. And pretty. And smart. And even if you're not popular, you're still nice. And kind. And so many other good—and true—things!

## Struggle

When I was a little girl, I felt like no matter what I did or how hard I tried, it just wasn't good enough. I was a *complete* perfectionist—and I was painfully self-aware. I was always wondering what people were thinking or saying about me. So many times, all of my "I'm-not-good-enough" thoughts washed over me like a waterfall. That can make life really hard for someone who wants to please others and do everything right and make everyone happy.

When I became a teenager, I changed a lot—and that's totally normal. The words I was regularly telling myself also changed. They got worse!

I actually started calling myself names when I didn't measure up or when I made mistakes or when—in my mind—I said or did or even wore the wrong thing.

When I was 15—you know, the year before I was supposed to get my driver's license—I became legally blind due to a disease called retinitis pigmentosa. Even though I received that difficult news with grace and resolve (God alone made that possible!), this new development in my life opened the door for even more negative thoughts and confidence-destroying self-talk.

*I'm never going to be independent.*

*I am so awkward.*

*People are staring at me.*

*Guys will never want to date me.*

And statements like those just went on and on. Forget that waterfall of negativity washing over me! Now I was swimming in an *ocean* of self-criticism! I felt frustrated. I lacked confidence. And I struggled with insecurity.

But I didn't spend all of my teen years unhappy or depressed or miserable. On most days, I felt just fine. I was active and involved and had friends. I even eventually met a great guy and got married and had kids and a career and all that amazing stuff.

But until I sorted through the closet of my mind and tossed out everything that didn't fit or wasn't flattering—the destructive self-talk, the lies, the thoughts that weren't really helpful—I was never totally free to live my life the way God wanted me to live it or to experience the joy He wanted me to experience. I also wasn't really able to be *me*.

Because here's the truth: *What you think and say to yourself will impact the texture, color, and music of your life.*

The things you say to yourself—about yourself—will shape the life you live by shaping your friendships. Your use of your gifts and talents. Your studies. Your interests and pursuits. Your walk with God. Your relationships with your family. Even your future!

Words are extremely powerful—even (and maybe especially) the ones you speak to yourself.

That's why we're going to dive headfirst into this crazy-sounding business of talking to yourself. Because soul talk really does make a difference in your life.

When you speak truth to your soul—to the inner you—that's when you become the girl God wants you to be. That's when you become more comfortable in your own skin. That's when you're able to reach out to others and live an amazing life of confidence and grace and truth and beauty.

## Fill Your Closet with Truth

There are good ways to start your day.

- Waking up as soon as your alarm goes off.
- Having your clothes picked out the night before so you don't waste time figuring out what to wear.
- Placing your backpack or school bag right by the front door, loaded up and ready to go, and knowing that you completed your homework and studied for the day's tests or quizzes.
- Spending a few minutes getting ready for your day by reading a devotional or your Bible.
- Eating a healthy breakfast that will give you energy and make you feel good.

And then there are bad ways to start your day.

- Sleeping through your alarm.

- Digging through your dirty clothes basket for something—*anything!*—to wear because nothing in your closet seems right.

- Realizing you totally forgot to do your math homework—and having no clue where your math book even is.

- Checking your Instagram instead of talking to God.

- Skipping breakfast and realizing your stomach is going to growl and you're going to have a headache until the bell rings for lunch.

Can you guess which scenario leads to more awful self-talk, *what's wrong with me* thoughts, and feelings of insecurity?

Yep, it's the second scenario, that picture of total unpreparedness!

When you don't take the time to get ready ahead of time and do the things you need to do, you can be in for a rough day.

It's the same way with your thoughts. When you don't prepare the closet of your mind by filling it with truth, it fills up with negative thoughts, feelings of insecurity, lies, and confusing ideas. And when you're feeling down, it's easy to grab those junky feelings and beliefs...

*Everyone is always judging me.*

*I'm literally not going to be able to get through this day.*

*My life is just a mess...and it's not getting better.*

Yet none of those thoughts are even remotely true—and the accompanying feelings are never helpful!

Why is it so important to clean out your thought closet regularly?

*Because if you don't control your thoughts, your thoughts will control you.* And they'll control every single part of your day.

That's why you need to constantly monitor the feed of your own self-talk. That's why you need to keep scrolling through the words you're telling yourself. That's why you need to delete the negative blog posts and replace them with positive ones.

## Truth

Okay, by now you've probably admitted that you talk to yourself. And you might be the kind of girl who has a full-blown conversation with yourself right out loud. Or maybe you're more the say-it-under-your-breath type. But you do have those talks with yourself, right? We all do!

If you want to have the right kinds of things in your thought closet—if you want to fill those shelves and bins and hangers with gorgeous pieces that will always look and feel fabulous on you—you need to tell yourself the right kinds of things.

My favorite place to shop for those right kinds of things is the Bible. And telling myself the truths I've found in the pages of Scripture has turned my thought closet from a hot mess of items that don't fit right and will never look good on me to a picture-perfect display of gorgeous colors and styles that are just right for me.

Now, you'll find almost as many kinds of closets and preferences and styles and organizing techniques as you'll find people on this planet. And you'll also find all kinds of self-talk—both good and bad. Because the pages of the Bible are filled with real flesh-and-blood people, you'll see it there too. But did those people in the Bible talk to themselves like we do today? Did they experience fear and frustration and insecurity and doubt? You bet they did! Some of them were even recorded having conversations with themselves. Keep reading and you'll see!

# *Wise Words*

It's interesting to read some of the words people stored in their thought closets long ago. Here's a sampling of wise words that filled the closets of people way back in Bible times:

- "Awake, my soul!" (Psalm 57:8).

- "My soul...put your hope in God" (Psalms 42:5,11; 43:5).

- "I have calmed and quieted my soul" (Psalm 131:2 NKJV).

- "O my soul...forget not all His benefits" (Psalm 103:2 NKJV).

- "Return to your rest, O my soul" (Psalm 116:7 NKJV).

- "O my soul, march on in strength!" (Judges 5:21).

- "Praise the LORD, O my soul" (Psalm 146:1 NKJV).

In modern-day language, these seven soul-talk statements might sound a little like this...

*Tune in.*
*Look up.*
*Calm down.*
*Look back.*
*Chill out.*
*Press on.*
*Lift up.*

Unlike our friends in the Bible, we don't usually make "O my soul" pronouncements aloud when we talk to ourselves. (That would be kind of weird if we did!) But we use silent words—a *lot* of silent words. Science proves it.

Psychologists and neuroscientists have discovered that everybody has a stream of self-talk that consists of between 150 and 300 words a minute. That's a lot of talking! In fact, that adds up to 45,000 to 51,000 thoughts each day. Most of these thoughts are the not-that-thrilling variety, like *Where did I leave my flip-flops?* or *What chapter of this book am I on?*

But another small yet powerful percentage of this self-talk is way more intense. These are thoughts that can be true or untrue. Helpful or unhelpful. Right or wrong. And they're about things that matter a whole lot more than where we put our flip-flops. I'm talking about the words we tell ourselves about who we are. About how much we matter. About what we think of ourselves. These are the words that directly affect how we live our lives.

Every day, we fill the closets of our minds one thought at a time, one silent word at a time, one comment at a time. Those powerful, life-changing thoughts and words and comments stay in our closets, and they're stored there for us to grab today or tomorrow or a year from now. Whenever we grab them and put them on, they influence both our feelings and our actions. The reality is this: Once in the closet, forever in the closet.

Unless we intentionally clean out that closet and replace less-than-helpful ideas and flat-out ugly lies with new words. Words of beauty. Words of encouragement. Words of truth.

By now you would probably agree that our words are powerful. Especially the words we say to ourselves. That's why we need to take a peek into the closets of our minds and see what's filling those shelves and bins and hangers.

And if your closet is a total disaster, don't worry about it. We can work with that!

## Crammed

Have you ever cleaned out your closet to get ready for a new season? You know, like packing away your winter clothes to make room for the spring and summer stuff. (Yay!) Or getting rid of things you've outgrown so you can fit your new back-to-school clothes in your closet. Whenever you do this, you probably discover a lot of things you're not totally in love with—and even some things that you've never, ever worn!

I remember going through my clothes one time after I moved and promising myself I would never again buy clothes I wasn't totally in love with just because they were on sale. I have this weird thing where I feel strangely attached to the stuff I buy, even though I might never wear it, just because it's *mine*. (Fuchsia and orange flowered pants, I'm talking about you!) I figure that once something is in my closet, it's forever in my life.

Our thought closets? Same. They're crammed with everything we've stuffed in them over the years. Some of it is cute and classy. But lots of it is ugly and unflattering. And because the items— the thoughts and words and comments—are *ours*, we can have a hard time getting rid of them.

Smart shoppers fill their closets with good pieces—clothes that fit well, are flattering, and will be worn again and again because they're cute and comfy and classic. We need to be smart shoppers when it comes to our thoughts. We need to choose wisely the things we say to our souls because all our self-talk gets shoved into the closet and stays there until we recall it. We need to speak truth to our souls so that it's truth that gets stored away and recalled. And truth always feels good and is in style! It's a wardrobe must-have!

## *Wardrobe Must-Haves*

What are the top ten items—clothes or accessories or both—on your wish list? These could be things you want for your birthday or Christmas or your back-to-school wardrobe. Write them down here:

1.

2.

3.

4.

5.

6.

7.

8.

9.

10.

Now, create a top ten list of true statements to and about yourself that you'd like to place in your thought closet. Or maybe it's easier to imagine some compliments you would love for someone to say to you. Either way, write down those encouraging truths right here:

1.

2.

3.

4.

5.

6.

7.

8.

9.

10.

. . . . . . . . . . . . . . . . . . . . . . . . . . .

Why did I want you to make that list? I'll explain.

When you're super busy with school and friends and activities, it's easy to forget things, isn't it? Things like homework. Or chores. Or taking your vitamins or putting in your retainer at night.

We forget the simplest things when we're busy, but when we're getting into our thought closets and sifting through what's in there, our minds are like steel traps. Nothing has been forgotten or misplaced. We have the unfortunate ability to remember all the wrong things at all the wrong times. Like a GPS, we can locate just the right memory of failure, the perfect insecurity, or the timeliest untruth—just when we *don't* need it most!

That's why we need to peek into the crammed closets of our minds and go through what's hanging and stuffed in there. As you sort through the contents, take the time to ask yourself a few questions about the specific thoughts and words and comments you find stored in your closet:

- *Do these thoughts and words and comments fill me with truth?*
- *Will the things stored in my closet help me live the life I want to live and be the person I want to be?*

If your answer to either of these questions is *no*, don't stress. Together, we're going to sort through your stuff and give away the negative so you'll have a whole wardrobe of the positive.

## Sort Through It

We've admitted that we talk to ourselves. And we've learned that some of the things we tell ourselves aren't very helpful. So the next thing we need to do is sort through all the thoughts and words and comments we already have stored in our minds. If something isn't a good fit, we can get rid of it. If something doesn't look good on us, we can toss it out. If something is stained or ripped or ruined, we can throw it away. We're only going to keep the good stuff.

And after we've gotten rid of the stuff we'll never wear, we're going to update our wardrobes. We're going to fill our closets with timely, attractive truths with which we can clothe ourselves—fashionable, well-fitting, freeing, and fabulous truths.

Romans 12:2 says, "Be transformed by the renewing of your mind."

The key word there is "renewing." And what's in the middle of that word? *New.* Instead of choosing our thoughts from a closet full of too-small, worn-out, not-in-style pieces, we're going to be choosing from an amazing selection of fits-just-right, classic, encouraging, joyful messages.

Girlfriend, you are a reflection of the way you think. Wise King Solomon put it this way: "As he thinks within himself, so he is" (Proverbs 23:7 NASB). Whatever you hang in your closet is what you will wear every day. It's what other people will see on you. It's often the first impression you make on others. And it's what you see in the mirror when you look at yourself.

Your soul talk will affect who you are.

Because your thoughts have such a major influence on your life, you can learn to control them—and sometimes change them—with some truthful soul talk. When you start thinking things that are true, you'll start believing them. When you stand in front of a mirror, you'll look at yourself with joy and contentment and a new amount of confidence. You'll be much more accepting of that girl who's staring back at you—that girl who is going to head for school or sports practice or play rehearsal with a light heart and a genuine smile. You'll be ready for whatever comes your way as you learn and grow and become the girl God created you to be.

If you keep a journal, this exercise makes for a great entry. You can look at the words from your thought closet and ask yourself, *Are these words I want to keep in my closet? Do I want to save them, or would it be better to let them go?* If you don't keep a journal, now would be a terrific time to start. You can write down all you're learning about yourself and about God, and you can start separating the truth from the lies.

When you say words of truth to yourself, you start living out that truth. Seriously! It really does work that way. So start speaking to yourself words of kindness. Words of truth that reflect who you really are. Words that make you feel just plain good about yourself and about the people around you. Words that affirm that you're God's much-loved daughter who's in the middle of a major thought-closet makeover!

## *THINGS TO THINK ABOUT*

- If you made a playlist of things you say to yourself, what would it sound like? Would the tone be upbeat? Sad? Angry? Something else? Or a combination? Why?

- Using terms you would use for clothes, describe the thoughts, words, and comments that are hanging in the closet of your mind. Also, are those thoughts, words, and comments giving you what you need to live the kind of life you want to live? Explain.

- What do you think God says in His Word about talking to yourself? We'll learn more about this later, but for now write down anything you can think of.

# KEEP OR TOSS?

Meredith sighed as she stared at the mess on her desk. Yesterday had been her last day of school, and all she wanted to do was sit on the couch, dive into a bag of her favorite potato chips, and watch Netflix. But she was leaving for soccer camp in two days, and before she left, her mom wanted Meredith to clean her desk. And not just clean off the surface. By *cleaning*, Meredith's mom meant doing all the icky stuff—totally emptying out her backpack, sorting through the school year's papers and books, recycling or tossing what she didn't need, and basically transforming her desk from looking like the aftermath of a tornado to *PBteen* photo-shoot-ready.

*Ugh!*

Meredith knew she'd feel better leaving for camp with a clean desk—not to mention a happy mom! Pulling out the recycling bin and grabbing spray cleaner and a cloth, she admitted to herself that it would have been so much easier to keep her desk clean in the first place.

*Too late now*, she grumbled. *Guess it's time to play the keep-or-toss game!*

Turning on her favorite playlist, Meredith began to tackle her overflowing binder. Halfway through the job, she was already starting to feel a little bit more motivated about the task. If she worked quickly, that bag of potato chips might still be there before her older brother got home from his summer job...

• • •

All of us have had to play the keep-or-toss game. If you're like Meredith—and like a lot of the rest of us!—you let things pile up until you *have* to deal with them. And then when it's time to get started, you have a huge mountain of stuff to sort through! Sitting on the couch with a bag of chips and zoning out in front of the TV sounds pretty good compared to the major task at hand.

So you may have the same thought Meredith did: *It would have been so much easier to keep things clean in the first place.*

Here's some good news though: You haven't had a whole bunch of years to let stuff pile up in your thought closet. The game of keep-or-toss is going to be *way* easier for you now than it would be if you started when you're 20. Or 30. Or 40. Or even older than that!

Right now, you can start looking at the thoughts, words, and comments that enter your mind and decide whether you should keep them.

A great guideline for doing this is Psalm 19:14: "Let the words of my mouth, and the meditation of my heart, be acceptable in thy sight, O Lord, my strength, and my redeemer" (kjv).

When we think of words that are acceptable to God, we tend to think of speaking the truth, saying "I'm sorry," or telling other people things that are going to make them feel good. We want the words we say to be kind and uplifting and honest. But Psalm

19:14 isn't just talking about the words we say to others. It also refers to "the meditation of my heart," which includes all the thoughts, words, and comments we tell *ourselves*. Our soul talk.

Some of the most powerful words we say are the words we speak to ourselves. The words no one else ever hears.

Just like we toss stuff onto our desks and it piles up, we toss into our thought closets words that would have been better dumped in the garbage. And it's hard *not* to do that. After all, we hear other girls constantly complaining about themselves and putting people down. That soundtrack for our lives makes negative words way too easy for us to grab, and most of the time, we don't even realize that we're grabbing them. And keeping them. And that one day we're going to have to deal with them.

Even though these negative words—most of which are actually complete lies—don't look good on us, we still dress ourselves in them because they've found shelf space in our thought closets. So when it's time to grab some words, we find them right there within easy reach. Often these words are so familiar—because we've heard them so many times from others or even from ourselves—that we use them without even thinking about what they're saying. And so we continue to tear ourselves down. We even find ourselves collecting other destructive thoughts and stashing them in the closets of our mind.

## Labels

You're probably all too aware of the social labels kids give each other. Popular. Loser. Nerd. Jock. Prep. You know, labels like those. Often, social labels dictate who you eat lunch with or hang out with after school. And a lot of the time, there isn't much mixing between the groups. You might actually click with people who are in another group, but you usually don't find out because the groups tend not to mix. And that means you miss out on some potentially good friends.

There are other types of labels besides social labels. Some are the labels we give ourselves—words we think fit us even though they really don't. Maybe it's hard for you to approach new people and talk to them. There's nothing wrong with that— lots of people are like that, actually—but you slap on yourself the label *shy* or *loner*. Or for some reason you're struggling with a particular school subject this year. You might just not be gifted in that subject, or maybe you have a poor teacher who's making the class harder than it needs to be. So you give yourself another label: *stupid*. Or you're not as good at gymnastics as your best friend is. Never mind that she's taken years and years of classes, plus takes private lessons, and you're pretty new to the sport. On goes another label: *unathletic*.

Do you see the danger here? These labels are lies. Read that sentence again: These labels are lies. But they pop up whenever we compare ourselves to other people and find ourselves—in that moment, in that situation, in our own minds—falling short. And in that moment we throw even more lying thoughts, words, and comments into our thought closets without really considering where they came from or if they even belong in the closet!

If that doesn't seem too bad, imagine walking down the street and finding a disgustingly filthy pair of jeans hanging out of a trash can. Would you pick up those jeans, take them home, and immediately put them in your closet without stopping to consider where they came from and without even washing them? No way!

And yet that's what we do with labels and lies and putting-ourselves-down words. And believe it or not, doing that is worse than putting into your closet those nasty jeans from the trash can. We're not just taking a mucky piece of clothing and adding it to our wardrobe. We're taking dirty, ill-fitting words and storing them in our hearts and minds that God values so highly.

Without really thinking about it, we borrow unbecoming

beliefs from other people and hang them in our thought closets. We grab random words and stuff them on the closet shelf without bothering to look at them first and see if they're true or false. We slap labels on ourselves without even bothering to see if they fit us.

So what can we do about our thought closets? How do we keep them clean? How can we keep them from looking like the surface of Meredith's desk? And finally, when it is time to clean and sort and organize, how do we even begin?

## Look for the Lies

A good place to begin the keep-or-toss game is with a great Bible verse in the New Testament. The apostle Paul was writing to a group of new Christians who were trying to figure out which teachings were true and which were lies. He told them to be constantly "fitting every loose thought and emotion and impulse into the structure of life shaped by Christ" (2 Corinthians 10:5 MSG).

Clearly, Paul expected everyone to have control of their own thoughts. That's why he called us to train our thoughts to match up with truth. We need to know what the truth is—something we do by reading God's Word and learning more about God—and then we need to be able to recognize ideas that don't line up with truth. As we get to know what truth looks like, we'll more easily be able to spot the lies.

Now let's get back to that idea of labeling. Those labels like *shy, loner, stupid,* or *unathletic* that we slap on ourselves can greatly affect our lives. Those words can make us feel different from others—and less than. Less important. Less valued. Less gifted.

All of us have been given a negative label—or given ourselves one. All of us know what it's like to carry around those labels believing that they actually describe us.

## *The Label Game*

As you identify labels you've worn, consider these lies: *dummy, idiot, ugly, lazy, fat, unpopular.* There are also those less-obvious labels, the "I'm not as good as" variety: *I'm not as good at math as my little sister. I'm not as pretty as my best friend. My clothes aren't as nice as the girls in the popular group. I'm not as talented as my brother. I'm not as fast as my teammate.*

Once you think of some negative labels you've worn, write them down here:

Now, cross them out and replace them with positive and true labels: intelligent, perceptive, cute, determined, healthy, friendly. Write them down here:

*These* are your designer labels, and they're the looks that really work for you. Go ahead and try them on. Then look in the mirror and see how great they look on you!

Once you've attached a negative label to yourself, it's pretty hard to shake it off. It's always in the back of your mind—when you're taking a test, when you're eating lunch with friends, when you're at dance class—even if you don't realize it's there. Or maybe you haven't thought about it in months and then—*boom!*—a negative label is in the forefront of your mind, making you feel frustrated or sad or angry.

That's why it's so, so important to take control of your thoughts. Meredith was about to finally take control of her desk, and you are about to take control of your negative thoughts about yourself. The great news is that you have all the cleaning supplies you need to play the game of keep-or-toss—and win!

## Tune in the Truth

When you're looking for lies, the best plan of attack is to become really familiar with the truth. It's like a song you hear that's not being performed by the original artist. You've heard the original so many times—especially if it's your current favorite song—that you know right away when you hear it being sung by a different singer.

Similarly, the better you get at tuning in to the truth, the better you get at recognizing the lies and tuning them out. Tossing out those wrong thoughts, words, and comments will become easier—and you'll eventually be able to see them as lies right away and not stuff them into your thought closet in the first place.

When wrong thoughts fly into your mind, you'll be able to take control of them and replace negative and untrue statements with positive truths.

*Hey*, you'll be able to tell yourself. *You're not an idiot. You're not a reject. You're not stupid. You're smart. And a good friend. And creative. Those negative labels are lies. And the positive labels are the things that are actually true about you.*

Here's the biggest truth of all: You are the workmanship of God. And He never makes anything that can be given a negative label. *Never.*

Sure, you can still get frustrated with yourself. You can still make mistakes and be upset about them. But you are *not* your frustrations or your mistakes. And you are *not* the negative thoughts that come along with those frustrations and mistakes. When you're familiar with truth's tune, you have the valuable ability to grab onto any negative, untruthful thoughts, words, and comments and refuse to let them into the closet of your mind. You have the power to say, "Hey, these things don't fit! They don't look good on me, I don't like them, and I have no use for them." And then you leave them right there—out of your mind and out of your life.

Now, I'm not saying this is an easy thing to do. It's definitely not! Especially when you're surrounded by images of perfection in the media and peers who tend to tear down themselves—and each other. Tuning in to the truth requires a lot of prayer and effort and wisdom.

And wisdom doesn't necessarily mean having a 4.0+ GPA or perfect SAT scores. It means being tuned in to God and His Word, always willing to listen to His leading, and always learning from life experiences. Wisdom is a very good thing to have when you're talking to yourself and deciding whether to store those thoughts, words, and comments in the closet of your mind.

When you talk to yourself, do you choose wise words? Are they words that your loving God would approve of? Are the words of your soul talk like life-giving water, or do they drain away your joy and I've-got-this confidence, leaving you thirsty and exhausted?

Words matter. And wise words totally matter! Because words matter so much, we can't risk speaking untruths to ourselves because we are likely to believe them.

## *Words, Words, Words*

Did you know that the average female speaks approximately 25,000 words a day? (And if we count all of the texting and posting and tweeting, the number is probably much higher!) That 25,000, though, counts only the words we speak out loud. We actually say way more than 25,000 words to ourselves, so you can only imagine what the grand total might be each day. It doesn't matter if our words are spoken aloud, texted to a friend, or said in the quiet of our own minds. All of them can be stored in our thought closets—if we let them. And if we keep them in the closet, all those words sit there, some helpful, many not; some true, and many not. Those lingering words can influence who we are and how we act and even who we'll eventually become. So choose wisely the words you speak to yourself and the words you store in your thought closet!

## What Truth Sounds Like

Remember how we talked about recognizing that a song isn't the real thing because you've heard the original so many times? It's like that with truth. We want to have heard the original so many times, over and over and over again, that we recognize a bad cover—a lesser imitation—as well as outright lies.

I've found that one of the best ways to recognize the truth is to know the words of Jesus. And we know them by reading them and hearing them over and over and over again.

It's amazing to consider the way Jesus used words, to listen to what wisely spoken truth sounds like. There's a story told in the Gospel of Luke that gives us a good picture of how Jesus spoke and how His words affected others.

Jesus had gone back home to Nazareth for a visit, and He stood in the synagogue on the Sabbath to teach. After Jesus finished speaking, "All spoke well of him and were amazed [or astonished] at the gracious words that came from his lips" (Luke 4:22).

Jesus's words were *gracious*. Kind. Pleasant. Courteous. Considerate. Thoughtful. Friendly.

Isn't that the way you want others to speak to you? Isn't that the way you want to speak to others? And isn't that the way you want to speak to yourself? *Words that are gracious.*

A few verses and several cities later, we see Jesus again hanging out in a synagogue on the Sabbath. This time He's in Capernaum. Different city, but same Jesus. The people here "were amazed at his teaching, because his words had authority" (Luke 4:32).

There's that word again: "amazed."

And now we learn that Jesus wasn't known only for His gracious words but also for His authoritative—or dependable, trustworthy, authentic, and accurate—speech. Wouldn't you love to be known for that—for being thoughtful and trustworthy, authentic and amazing? Sounds good to me!

God's truth is always authoritative and gracious. And even though "authoritative" might give us an image of a super-strict teacher who never smiles and always hands out harsh punishments, according to the Bible, authoritative words should never be harsh. And "gracious" might sound like you just let things go or quickly give up, but real grace has real power.

So ask yourself this: Are the words you speak to yourself gracious? Are they kind? Or are they harsh? And—most of all—are they truthful? Do they place God's truth in your heart?

I know I'm speaking this truth over and over and over again, but let's review. The words you speak to yourself are important even though nobody else hears them or can be hurt by them. But someone *is* listening. *You* are listening. And, sweet girl, *you* can be hurt by the words you say to yourself. Whatever you say to yourself—things that are true and things that are lies—have the same impact, for good or for bad, as the words you say to others or the words they say to you.

I had a really interesting conversation with a "professional talker" (yep, such a thing really exists!) about this exact thing. Marilyn Meberg is a professional talker—a licensed therapist (like a counselor), an author, and a professional speaker. Here's how Marilyn described her own self-talk:

> **JENNIFER:** Do you ever speak to yourself with self-condemnation? If you do something stupid, do you ever say, *Marilyn, you knucklehead!*
>
> **MARILYN:** (Laughs) A million times.
>
> **JENNIFER:** But not to the extent that it's a real problem?
>
> **MARILYN:** (Laughs even louder) *Of course* to the extent that it's a problem! But when I speak to myself that way, sometimes I need to hear that. Sometimes I've done a dumb thing, a tactless thing, something that is lacking wisdom. And I will chastise myself, and I need to hear that sometimes. It's like a parent has to discipline a child: I discipline myself. *Now, Marilyn, you could avoid that next time if you would just...*

**JENNIFER:** So you *counsel* yourself?

**MARILYN:** I take myself into my office and I have a chat. And when I come out of the office, I either want my money back, or I'll say, *You know, that was good.* That's constructive, not condemning, though. As you know, some levels of self-condemnation are damaging.

**JENNIFER:** How do you know the difference?

**MARILYN:** Oh, sometimes I need the correction. Sometimes I need the discipline. Sometimes I need to own the truth. That's instruction. That's good for me. That builds me up. But when I feel condemned, like I'm not good enough, that's not *in*structive. That's *de*structive. Instruction brings life; condemnation brings destruction.

Did you catch that? As Marilyn taught so clearly, wise, truthful words are never harsh or unkind. They are gracious. Wise and truthful words are never wimpy or without power. They have authority. But even the hard truths we speak to ourselves should not be condemning. They should build us up. Like Marilyn, we can and should counsel ourselves with the truth. But if you counsel yourself too harshly, you should demand your money back!

Proverbs 18:21 says something pretty intense: "The tongue has the power of life and death." Wow! Life and death? That's pretty weighty. Your words can bring life—both to you and to others—or they can begin a downward spiral. They can build up with truth and joy. Or they can tear down with lies and bitterness. That's why it's so important to choose your words wisely!

And remember, this is not just about the words you speak to other people. Or the texts you send. Or the updates you post. It's about the words, thoughts, and comments that travel the short distance from *you* to *you*.

Think about it this way. Would you tolerate someone else speaking to you the way you sometimes speak to yourself? If your BFF called you an idiot (and she wasn't joking) when you spilled your Starbucks on her sweatshirt, you'd feel horrible, wouldn't you? Yet "idiot" might be the first word you speak to yourself when you spill something. And it doesn't matter if you say it silently or out loud. It has an impact—a negative impact—either way.

Clearly, calling someone—even yourself—an idiot is not gracious or based on the authority of Scripture. It is not instructive; it is destructive. I can't afford to hang that untruth in my closet, and neither can you. But a name we brutally call ourselves is too easy to keep and too hard to toss out when we're not tuned in to the truth.

## Word Count

As a student, you're probably all too aware of word counts. Whether you're writing a long paper or a short one, you need to make sure you hit the word count assigned by your teacher, right? You need to pay attention to know if you've written too much or too little. And as girls prone to talking to ourselves, we need to be just as aware that our words—the words we say to ourselves—*count*. We could totally benefit from paying the same attention to the words we say to ourselves as the words we write down in an essay for school.

Basically, we write down words on the surfaces of our own minds and hearts when we speak to ourselves.

If you tend to talk to yourself a lot (and—let's be honest here—what girl doesn't?), remember that what you say matters. The next time you gear up to fire off some choice words to your soul, stop and consider the words of Paul: "Let your conversation be gracious and attractive so that you will have the right response for everyone" (Colossians 4:6 NLT).

Pay close attention to the words you say when you're talking to yourself. Are the words you're saying true? How would you feel if someone else said those words to you? Can you imagine God saying them to you?

Cleaning a messy desk and sorting through a school year's worth of accumulated belongings wouldn't be the highlight of any girl's summer vacation. But you'll never enjoy your summer break if you have a big mess and an unfinished project constantly hanging over you. Sure, you can cover that messy desk with a beach towel or blanket and try to pretend that it doesn't exist, but that doesn't get rid of the heaping pile. It's still there, demanding your attention.

Same with your thought closet. There's no way to close the door and completely ignore all those unsightly and harmful thoughts, words, and comments. Like the pile on your desk, those words own you as long as you allow them to stay there. That's why it's essential that you start to do something—some type of cleaning or sorting or organizing—a little at a time. That's why you need to get going on the keep-or-toss game.

There's one more thing I want to let you know as we prepare to fill our thought closets with words that are beautiful and true. You might never be able to erase 100 percent of the old memories, destructive thoughts, or negative words you've said to yourself. But your good and powerful God can make them so they don't matter anymore.

And, in the power of His Spirit living within us, we can clean out the items in our thought closets. We can get rid of the old wardrobe that hangs there. We can toss the lies and replace them with truth. We can get rid of anything old and unflattering and not cool and replace those things with the lovely and always-in-fashion words of God's truth.

Are you ready to sort through the stuff in your thought closet, get rid of what you don't want anymore, and make room for words that will totally work for you? I know I am. Let's get going!

## *THINGS TO THINK ABOUT*

- What sits on your shelves and hangs out in your thought closet? Just list the things in plain sight. We don't need to dig too deep right now. Which of these things should you keep? Why? Which should you toss? Why?

- What are the three thoughts you think about yourself most frequently? Don't think about it too hard. Just write down what pops into your mind right away. In what ways is thinking these thoughts affecting how you act, what you say, and how you feel?

- Are most of the things in your thought closet based on truth or lies? Why do you think that is?

- Do you sometimes call yourself names? Are they names you would want other people to call you? Think of new names—positive, true, affectionate nicknames—you can call yourself instead of calling yourself something negative by default. (If you can't think of anything, ask your mom or dad or BFF for ideas. They'll have plenty!) Write down these better options so you can remember them when you're searching for something positive to say to yourself.

# 3

# PERFECTLY IMPERFECT

Alexis held her breath as she waited for the website to upload her final grades. Okay, here they were...English: A. History: A-. Biology: B+. Art: A-. Geometry: A-. French: B.

So much for her perfect GPA. She knew it had been a tough semester—she'd had a long bout with the flu, some of her teachers were really hard, and her beloved Grammy had passed away—but only one solid A in the bunch? Not good! What were her parents going to say? Alexis's big sister, Brooke, kept a 4.0 all through high school. True, Brooke hadn't had Alexis's crazy schedule—swim practice before *and* after school, first-chair cellist in the school orchestra, kids' group leader at church—but Alexis figured her mom and dad would be disappointed in her anyway.

When she finally shared the news with her parents, though, Alexis got the surprise of her life.

"Honey," her dad said, "we know that you did your best— especially considering how sick you were this spring and the grief you were dealing with after losing Grammy. You're smart, you're a hard worker, and you have so many other talents and gifts that a report card doesn't reflect."

"You mean you don't expect me to be perfect?" Alexis grinned. "Wow! This takes all the pressure off for next year. I'm not going to try at all!"

Her mom instantly gave her a look of disapproval.

"Kidding!" Alexis grinned. "But honestly, you have no idea how much better this makes me feel—knowing I don't have to be perfect!"

• • •

Like it or not, a lot of things in your life can be measured and judged by how "perfect" you seem. A 4.0 GPA, a "10" in gymnastics, a piano recital with no mistakes, an impressive number of followers on social media…even having clear skin and wearing trendy clothes can be considered standards of perfection. All this pressure for perfection can drive a girl crazy, right?

So it should come as no surprise that many of the words we tell ourselves are a result of this pressure to be perfect. Alexis may have called herself stupid or lazy after seeing her grades. If you break out with acne at that time of the month, you might be tempted to call yourself ugly. If your gymnastics all-around score is lower than you hoped for, you could throw a few more negative words into your thought closet, like "clumsy" or "loser." But none of these things are true.

We're imperfect—*all* of us are imperfect—but we're tempted to believe lies about ourselves anytime we find ourselves falling short of perfection. And this means that we're always going to be tempted to believe lies because we're always going to be imperfect.

## Wrong Assumptions

As a little girl on my way to church each Sunday, I rode with my family past a beautiful Catholic church. The stately, ornate building itself was gorgeous. But one day something I saw totally blew me away: an ordinary street sign was planted in the parking lot of this extraordinary church. And, you know what it said?

It read "Angle Parking Only."

I was only about six or seven years old, and I wasn't the best reader. I thought the sign read "*Angel* Parking Only."

I just couldn't believe the Catholics had angels attending their services. Wow. I certainly had never seen any at my church!

Not until many years later did I realize my reading goof. It was fun imagining that angels had places to park at the Catholic church, but I was totally wrong about that.

My thinking was based on my imperfect reading ability. I read *angles* as *angels*. And from there my imagination took off— and those wondrous imaginings were all based on a completely wrong assumption.

When I was in school, I had a lot of wrong assumptions. As a result, I filled my thought closet with a lot of destructive thoughts, words, and comments. Things like *No matter how hard you try, you always could have done better.* I totally believed that my worth and my acceptance by other people were determined by how well I performed. (My self-image definitely was!) I was constantly measuring myself against the scale of perfection.

Because of this, I had a lot of junk taking up space in my thought closet that didn't fit and didn't look good on me. Stuff I should have tossed. But I had chosen to clothe myself with wrong thinking. And those misguided thoughts grew into unrealistic expectations. As you can imagine, this mindset affected the way I saw myself and the way I assumed other people saw me. All I saw were my glaring imperfections, and I wasn't very patient with myself. Or forgiving. Or loving.

And because I was so focused on my less-than-perfect self, I lived as if life were all about me. I assumed everyone was staring at me and noticing all my imperfections when in reality they weren't paying any attention to me at all. (That's because they were too busy being concerned about their own imperfections!)

We live by what we assume, by how we believe things are. Sometimes we're right, but a lot of the time we're wrong. We don't see ourselves accurately. We think we've read the sign correctly—like my "Angel Parking Only" sign—but we actually misread it. And what we assume—what we believe to be true—affects our thoughts and, eventually, our actions.

## Root and Fruit

Here's another way to understand this idea of wrong assumptions. Think of a plant that grows fruit—like a cherry tree or a raspberry bush. Our assumptions—the things we believe to be true—are the root, and our thoughts are the fruit. The root of wrong thinking is always lies. The root of right thinking is always truth.

Imagine you've just landed on our planet right in the middle of a lush orchard, thick with a variety of trees. How would you determine what kinds of trees you saw?

By the fruit growing on them. (Okay, I'm assuming you're a very cute alien familiar with fruit, but you get the point!)

You could dig down to cut a sample from the root system or perhaps take some kind of core sample from deep within the trunk of the tree. But the most practical way to find out what kind of tree you were looking at would be to examine its fruit.

So what kind of fruit is growing on your tree? Maybe you're overly sensitive to what other people say. I'm familiar with this bad-tasting fruit. I got very good at constantly interpreting other people's words and actions as judgments on me. Even if what they were saying and doing weren't meant to be.

Or you might be overly self-aware. The root of this fruit is pride. Basically, you're way too tuned in to yourself and not tuned in enough to others. An unhealthy level of self-awareness might be common in our culture, but it's not fruit you want to cultivate in your life. It's just plain gross!

And then there's that fruit we talked about at the beginning of this chapter: perfectionism. Nothing you do is good enough because someone, somewhere, is always doing it better. The poisonous fruit of perfectionism springs from the root of low self-esteem or insecurity.

Remember, in all of these things—being overly sensitive or unhealthily self-aware or an unrelenting perfectionist—a wrong assumption is the root, and the wrong thinking is the fruit. We *assume* other people are judging us. We *assume* life is all about us. We *assume* we aren't supposed to make any mistakes. And then we start thinking that way.

It's like Alexis assuming she was supposed to have the same GPA her sister had. And Alexis started thinking that way. She became anxious about her grades and what her parents might think—when actually, she later learned, she didn't have anything to worry about. But her wrong assumptions directed her thinking. And in her thought closet she stored untrue words about herself that she never should have bought into in the first place, much less kept.

## Digging

We don't experience negative feelings like insecurity, anger, intolerance, or defensiveness unless something feeds those feelings or thoughts. Remember the root and fruit? Our feelings and thoughts are the *fruit*. Wrong assumptions are the *root* that feeds—among other negative feelings—insecurity, anger, intolerance, and defensiveness. Changing that fruit is impossible without changing the root.

Which means we're going to need to put on our hot-pink, very attractive gardening gloves, grab a shovel, and do a little digging.

If we want to cultivate the right kind of fruit—like contentment and joy and kindness and confidence—we need to figure out whether our assumptions are true or false. If they're true, we can continue to give them sunlight and water and encourage them to grow. But if they're false, we need to cut them off at the root so they don't bear any fruit in our lives. Even better, we can dig out that root!

You do this by simply calling something what it is. Insecurity? Its root is a lie. Perfectionism? A total lie is at its root! Overly sensitive to criticism? That's also rooted in a lie.

*Calling* something what it is helps you more clearly *see* and then remember it for what it is. So if it's a root you need to get rid of—a root that's being fed and watered by lies—choke that root out with the truth. Speak words of truth and beauty and kindness to yourself. Not perfect? So what? Neither am I, and neither is anyone else. Focus on another fruit—a positive fruit, like your work ethic or enthusiasm or creativity.

## Garden of Truth

Start growing a garden rooted in truth—a garden that's going to yield some delicious fruit. Think of some good "root" words for your garden that describe yourself. Like fun. Compassionate. Accepting. Happy. Write them down here:

Now, go out in the world and share the fruit of your garden with others!

When you discover your own root—one that's based in truth—you begin to experience freedom and confidence. You also gain knowledge and understanding when you tend the garden of your life—when you try something new, when you learn, and even when you fail. When you figure out your root, you're able to focus on the fruit.

Learning to identify the roots of your thoughts about yourself is so important to figure out right now—while you're a lovely young woman with a bright future. You are too valuable and life is too precious for you to live according to wrong assumptions. That's why you need to dig down and make sure the roots of your life are planted in God's truth. When you base your life and your beliefs on what is right and true, the fruit of your life will show it. And to figure out what is right and true, you need to gain wisdom.

## Wise Up

Have you ever woken up mad at your BFF or a sibling after dreaming that he or she did something really mean to you? *How could he do such a thing? How could she say that? It totally doesn't seem possible!*

Then your brain unfogs, and you realize it was all just a dream. But the crazy thing is that it felt so *real*. That's what wrong assumptions are like. They feel so real, but that doesn't mean they're right or true.

In real life, have you ever made a wrong assumption based on false info? Maybe you assumed someone was a snob—but then you found out she was just shy. Or you assumed someone was mean—but then you found out he was just having a really bad day. Or you assumed someone was being unfair—but once you heard the other side of the story, you realized your assumption was wrong.

We all do this. All of us can be quick to make judgments and form opinions and slap on labels. So how do we get out of the habit of doing this? How can we make sure that we're rooted in the truth? Let me give you three surefire ways to gain the wisdom you need to recognize truth, right assumptions, and healthy fruit.

## Request Wisdom

The first thing to do is to ask God for wisdom. He knows that we need His knowledge, and He's ready and willing to give it to us. The Bible tells us, "If any of you lacks wisdom, you should ask God, who gives generously to all without finding fault, and it will be given to you" (James 1:5).

It's that simple. Just ask God for wisdom—and trust that He will give it to you. It's like going to a restaurant and asking for a glass of water. You trust that the server will bring you the water. It's a logical request for something good, and there's not really any reason your request wouldn't be granted.

Sometimes it's tempting to ask for perfection instead of wisdom. Of course, you might not come right out and say, "God, please make me perfect." But you basically ask that when you pray for things like getting 100 percent on your math test or first place in your track meet. It's better, though, to ask God for wisdom for your situation and that His will be done in your life, even if that means you don't end up with perfect results. It's better to ask Him to teach you—whatever the results—how to be more like Him.

When we ask God for wisdom, He responds big-time. He doesn't just give us a little sprinkling of it. He dumps it out! And it's our job to recognize it and use it in our lives. One of God's favorite things to do is to lavish on us wisdom that will benefit us and those around us.

God makes the attainment of wisdom as simple as asking for it. Just as simple as requesting a glass of water in a restaurant or asking your mom to "please pass the potatoes" at the dinner table. Amazing! And God gives us an overflowing supply of wisdom when we do ask.

King Solomon in the Bible knew this truth. He wrote, "The LORD gives wisdom; from his mouth come knowledge and understanding" (Proverbs 2:6). So I'll repeat it one more time because it's such a big deal: Ask God for wisdom and trust Him to provide. I promise that He will!

### Revere God

You can also receive wisdom by choosing to revere—or show great respect for—God. The Bible tells us, "The fear of the LORD is the beginning of wisdom, and knowledge of the Holy One is understanding" (Proverbs 9:10).

What comes to mind when you think of fearing someone or something? Maybe being afraid of a mean teacher? Or a vicious dog? Or a scary situation? That's not the kind of fear the Bible is talking about here. God doesn't want us to see Him as we would see a vicious dog or the dark woods. That wouldn't make for a very good relationship with Him, would it?

We don't need to feel that kind of fear of God, because He is good and kind. But He is also holy, perfect, sovereign, and worthy of our highest regard and respect. To fear the Lord means we approach Him and speak to Him with respect. We also need to act toward God as we would act toward a king who invited us into his royal chamber. (Just imagine your favorite good king from a Disney movie or your favorite book, and then imagine God being so much wiser and kinder and better than that!) We would totally be aware of this earthly king's high position, especially compared to our lowly one. How much more aware we are to be of God's high and holy position!

Now is a great time to take a look at your own heart and mind. Do you fear the Lord—in a good way? When it comes to making decisions or figuring out what's important in your life, whose truth do you depend on? Your own? Our culture's? Or God's?

Be honest with yourself here. It's super easy to start believing that the things you see online or on TV or among your peers are true and important. And it's easy to let those perceived truths and false values affect your thoughts and opinions and choices and actions. But just because you've seen or heard something a million times doesn't necessarily mean it's true or good for you.

## Get Real

Take a few minutes to page through the ads in a magazine or scroll through images on Pinterest or Tumblr. As you do this, write down some myths that you see illustrated: perfectly clear skin, a spotless bedroom, too-white teeth. Are these things real? Or have the photos had a little help on the editing end? After you make your list, write in big letters over the top, "Nobody's Perfect!" Then get out there and start living your wonderful, crazy, beautiful, and imperfect life.

And what about your friends and peers? Because you're with them so much, it's natural to notice their language and way of thinking and the way they dress...and then start adopting those things as your own habits. But are their ways good? Are they true? Are they things God wishes you to adopt for yourself? Take a few moments to talk to God about those things. Could it be you're just trying to be like everyone else and doing your best to fit in?

These are hard questions—and your honest answers might not be easy to accept. But God knows you're truly trying to honor and follow Him, and He will help you figure these things out. When you reverence God, when He is more important than anyone or anything else in your life, when you acknowledge that He is the standard of truth...that's when you'll find true wisdom.

. . . . . . . . . . . . . . . . . . . . . . . . . . . . .

### Receive Counsel

You'll also gain God's wisdom through counsel—through the advice, influence, and guidance of someone who's tuned in to the Lord and walking solidly with Him. Especially at your age, it's incredibly important that you have godly mentors and friends in your life. The book of Proverbs (which is overflowing with wisdom, by the way!) advises us that "wisdom is with those who receive counsel" (13:10 NASB), and "the wise of heart will receive commands" (10:8 NASB). When we walk with people like this, their wisdom rubs off on us—in a totally good way.

Do you know someone who can share godly wisdom and counsel with you? Maybe it's your mom. Or your big sister. Or your youth leader. Or a summer camp counselor you've kept in touch with. I totally recommend finding an older female ("older" meaning at least a few years older than you) who is solid in her walk with God and asking her to be your mentor. It might be a little bit scary to ask—it's always hard to put yourself out there like that—but you'll be so glad you did! You can meet together once a week or so for lunch or froyo or Starbucks and just talk about how you're doing with whatever's going on in your life. And you can pray together. Trust me, having a mentor is amazing!

My favorite mentors have shared their life experiences with me and helped me understand what true, helpful, and encouraging words I should tell myself.

Author Patsy Clairmont—who has written some really terrific books that have helped me a ton—once told me that when she talks to herself, she sounds like a cheerleader. That image really stuck with me! When I asked Patsy why she did this, she answered, "Because it's my tendency to be extremely critical, especially of myself. In fact, I'm far harder on myself than I am on others." And that's true for most of us—or maybe all of us!

Patsy also told me how she once realized that the words she was telling herself were mainly negative, but the words she was hearing from everyone else about her were pretty much all positive. She told me, "I had to stop and say, *Everyone can't be wrong. Do I trust their judgment? And do I think they are wise? Am I willing to receive what they are saying as truth? If I am, then I have to change the messages inside me.*"

Sometimes we just need to listen to others, learn from their mistakes and experiences, and recognize that they struggle the same way we do. Other people can teach us a lot if we take the time to listen. And that's where a mentor is so helpful.

Think about older girls and women in your life who could possibly be a mentor to you. Is there someone you know who seems wise? Someone who would be willing to walk with you so that you can gain wisdom? Someone who can share the truth she's basing her life on and the lessons she's learned? Pray that God will help you find that person—she is out there for you! And in the meantime, I'm here to keep walking with you through this book and teaching you the best way to talk to yourself.

## Back to Wisdom

But let's get back to wisdom for just a minute. You'll become well acquainted with a mentor once you spend time with her and get to know her. In the same way, you'll become well acquainted with wisdom when you simply request it (like asking for a glass of water in a restaurant), when you reverence God (like you would honor and respect a really good king), and when you receive wise counsel (from the Bible, from your parents, or from a special mentor). When you do these things, wisdom will become one of your best friends. How much of a best friend? Like this: "Say to wisdom, 'You are my sister,' and call understanding your intimate friend" (Proverbs 7:4 NASB).

I love that. If wisdom were truly your sister, what would she say to you during a sleepover? If understanding happened to be your BFF, what would she say to you when you were getting smoothies after school?

You can count on one thing. You wouldn't want to miss a single word of that sister and friend!

Remember, having wisdom doesn't mean being perfect. When we get tricked into believing that we need to be perfect—which is impossible—we miss out on going after the things we could and should be pursuing in this life. Things like God's wisdom. And His understanding. And His plan for our lives.

The Bible tells us that wisdom is more valuable than gold. And wisdom helps you know what to say when you talk to yourself.

> The hearts of the wise make their mouths prudent,
> and their lips promote instruction (Proverbs 16:23).

So be patient with yourself. Accept that you're not perfect. That's something all of us have in common—we are imperfect. Also, when you start to get overly critical of yourself or begin tossing negative words, thoughts, and comments into your thought closet, remember the image of the root and the fruit. If the root is based on lies, the fruit won't be good. But if the root is based on truth, the fruit will be delicious and totally worth the effort to grow it.

If you sprinkle God's rich wisdom on the soil of your life, you'll ensure that the roots are healthy, and you'll soon begin to see beautiful fruit. True, not every piece of fruit on a tree will be perfect, but there will be so much goodness on the tree of your life that everyone will notice! And did you know that by speaking wisely to your soul, you'll be able to shrivel some of those old, sickly roots (you know, the ones based on lies)? That wise speaking will further nourish the good roots—the ones based on truth—that may be struggling to take hold.

So don't expect perfection with yourself, but do go after wisdom with all you've got. Roots are strong, but with wisdom, you are stronger. If you apply the strength of truth to your wrong assumptions, you'll be able to get rid of any bitter, sour fruit in your life—the kind you spit out. And you'll taste the sweet deliciousness of perfectly ripened fruit. Yummy!

## THINGS TO THINK ABOUT

- What are some of the fruits in your life that don't taste very good, fruits you'd like to get rid of?

- Can you identify the roots of those fruits? If you were to dig down to their roots, what truths or lies would you find? Be specific.

- What can you do to resist the world's standards of perfection? What are some of the ways you can search for and discover God's wisdom?

- What's your "fear factor"—do you fear God, revering Him in a healthy way? As you draw closer to the God of the Bible, your awe of Him will grow. Read Psalm 23 and the Gospel of John to get started. Also, ask God to reveal Himself in your life.

- If you don't have a godly mentor, think of some older girls and women in your life whom you admire. Pray about asking one of them to be a mentor to you—and then follow through.

# 4

# TUNE IN

*Where is my costume?* Kendall frantically yanked clothes off hangers and rummaged through the shelves and baskets in her closet. She had to leave for her dance competition in ten minutes, and she had no idea where her tap costume had gone.

*Black tights...Oh, those have feet. I need to wear the kind without... Green sparkly dress... Nope, that's the turquoise one from jazz... Where in the world is my stuff?*

"Kendall, did you remember to put hairspray in the cart when you and Mom went shopping?" Kendall's little sister, Abigail, peeked her head into the room.

"Oh, no! I totally forgot!"

"Well, we're out, and we totally need some for competition. Are you almost ready? I'll fill your water bottle for you. We need to leave soon."

"My water bottle? Uh...I think I left it at the dance studio."

No costume. No hairspray. No water bottle. Kendall was a hot mess. How would she ever get to this competition on time...and if she did make it, would she even be able to remember her dance?

• • •

Doesn't it often seem that when one thing goes wrong, it's followed by another…and another…and another? And the whole time, you're constantly talking to yourself.

*Where did I put that book?*

*Did I leave my lunch at home again?*

*What did my friend mean by that comment?*

*How did I forget that we had a science test today?*

*Why won't he text me back?*

At times like this we need to stop talking, tune in, and listen.

## The Main Issue

A lot of the time, one specific thing in our life is actually the source of many of our other issues. A challenging teacher or class, or a hot-and-cold friend, or a general lack of self-confidence—an issue like these can spill out and affect many other parts of our lives. Like the rest of our classes. Or other friendships. Or other feelings we have inside. These bigger issues can even affect our health. If you're stressed out, you're much more likely to break out, lose sleep, and get sick.

For me, blindness is the defining thing that opens the door to a bunch of other bewildering issues. One of the biggest daily realities I've faced as a blind person is the stress of not being able to drive, read, or be independent. And stress, as you know, is totally not good for you.

Now back to our thought closets. You know how you make space for accessories—like scarves or necklaces or headbands—in your bedroom closet? Well, your issues come with accessories that take up room in your thought closet. And once they're in your closet, they tend to stay there. And new issues will constantly pile up on the shelves of your thought closet if you let them. And when the pile gets way too big, that's when you find yourself with a hot mess—like Kendall did when everything was piling up before her dance competition.

Sometimes you need a little more help than positive self-talk or being your own cheerleader. Kendall definitely needed some help getting it together so she could gather the things she needed and get out of the house on time. She could ask her mom to find her costume and accept her sister's offer to fill her water bottle. Like Kendall, we sometimes need a little help from an outside source. In addition to addressing our issue—that main problem we're dealing with—and practicing some healthy soul talk, we need to tune in to the true source of encouragement. And that source is faith in God.

## Have Some Faith

The Bible never says that our soul talk changes our situation and gives us hope. The God of the Bible is the one who changes our situation and gives us hope, and we invite Him in when we put our faith in Him. Faith in God enables us to see Him bring healing into our lives and help us get through the rough patches. Being your own cheerleader—giving yourself positive and encouraging messages—can contribute to your faith, but it doesn't replace it. And your faith grows when you speak truth to your soul—truth that comes directly from God.

By faith we receive truth. By faith we believe truth. And by faith we act on that truth.

Soul talk is faith's companion, not its replacement. Soul talk can't replace prayer either. Those are two very different things. If you feed yourself a steady stream of true thoughts, words, and comments, that's awesome, but it will never be the same as talking to God.

The things we're dealing with—a learning challenge, a relationship issue, family problems, a negative body image—can dictate our beliefs, color our actions, and affect our attitudes. But so can our faith! So it's important that we focus on the truth of Scripture and nurture our faith in Christ. Doing so helps us tell ourselves truth and put positive, hopeful ideas—attractive and well-fitting ideas—into our thought closets.

## My Story

If you're like me, you've had days when you're super busy and stressed out and have no idea how you're going to get everything done. Homework is piling up. Soccer practice in the afternoon. Mom's counting on you to babysit. Friends want to hang out. You need to log those volunteer hours for school. *Ugh!* you think. *I am so stressed. I am so overwhelmed, I can't even deal with it...It's just too much.*

Yep, I've been there, giving myself that kind of self-talk. Totally *not* being my own cheerleader! Talking to yourself about the stress you're feeling doesn't exactly make you want to jump out of bed, does it? But it's the truth: You're stressed out. Overwhelmed. Loaded down with too many demands on your life and your time—and you're still just a kid. I'm pretty sure you've felt like that. Who hasn't!

I've had the most amazing experience, though, and it's happened quite often. Sometimes in the morning, when I'm totally freaking out about my day, it's like a spotlight appears, illuminates my self-talk, and then changes the things I'm telling myself. I begin to focus on God, and then my thoughts go something like this: *God, You are sufficient. You are present. You are here with me. And I can do all things because You will give me Your strength!*

The difference is that I'm not talking to myself when I'm saying those things. I'm talking to God.

Sweet girl, when you shift your focus to God, you look away from your own thought closet that's stuffed with problems, and you are able to clearly see your Source of peace and comfort. Looking to God will reduce your stress level and help you get through the day.

A thought closet stuffed with negativity and lies can't give you anything helpful or true. You need a thought closet filled with thoughts rooted in the truth of Scripture. And we need this thought closet to be orderly and under control so it's easy for us to find the good stuff when we need it. When we're feeling hormonal and our emotions are overwhelming us, it's especially important that we choose only productive, healthy ideas from our thought closets. Otherwise we risk saying or doing something we'll totally regret. And we'll still be feeling stressed out and overwhelmed—probably more than ever, actually.

## Tune In to the Spirit

Have you ever been riding in the car for a while—maybe you're on a family vacation or driving to another town—and the only music you can get on the radio is either really fuzzy or lame! When this happens, you turn off the radio, right? You don't want to hear something that sounds terrible or music you just plain don't like. We need to do the same thing with our thoughts. We need to tune out what we know we shouldn't be hearing—untrue talk either from ourselves or from other people—and tune in to what is pleasing and good. And that is often the music of the Holy Spirit in your life.

Before Jesus went to heaven, He introduced His disciples to the coming Holy Spirit.

> When the Father sends the Advocate as my representative—that is, the Holy Spirit—he will teach you everything and will remind you of everything I have told you (John 14:26 NLT).

When we place our trust in Christ, when we have faith in Him, He gives us the gift of His Spirit to help us in this life. The Spirit fulfills several roles for us (I'll get to that in a minute), and as we rely on Him rather than on ourselves, He equips us to tell ourselves things that are healthy and helpful, encouraging and true. He helps us keep our thought closets tidy so we're able to find the good stuff right when we need it.

Jesus referred to the Holy Spirit as a Counselor, a representative of Christ, a Teacher, and One who would remind us of truth. Even with all those descriptions, you may find it hard to understand who the Holy Spirit is and what He wants to do in your life. So stick with me as I explain four of the Spirit's roles.

## Four Roles of the Spirit
### God's Spirit Counsels Us

When we're stressed out—like Kendall was right before her dance competition—it can be hard to know the right thing to do. And this is true for big problems as well as little ones—for everything from dealing with the sadness caused by your parents' divorce to being frustrated with your little brother being a pest. We can find ourselves overreacting or exploding or stuffing our feelings—any number of behaviors that aren't very healthy. That's when we need a Counselor.

Maybe your school has a counselor who is there to listen to students, help them with their problems, and connect them with others if they need a little more help. At first, visiting a counselor might seem intimidating, but it's a safe place to go if you need to talk to someone.

All of us need a Counselor, and God's Spirit is the perfect Counselor. He is safe. He is wise. He is fair. He is completely committed to our absolute good. And we can always trust Him to give us the best direction and never to lead us off course.

God's Spirit challenges us to hear truth, recognize it as truth, and apply that truth to our lives. He counsels us through His calm, quiet voice in our spirit.

You might be wondering why the Spirit's voice is so quiet. It would make more sense if it were loud, wouldn't it? Why doesn't He shout down the noise of our busy world? But that's not the way the Spirit works. He won't try to overshadow our distractions. To hear Him, we have to step away from the craziness of those distractions, quiet ourselves, and truly *listen*.

## Learn to Listen

Stop for a moment and write down everything you hear. Everything—the radio playing, the refrigerator humming, your sister sneezing. Notice how much you hear when you actually take time to stop and listen.

That was probably easy for you, but listening for the Holy Spirit's voice takes more practice. Sometimes when we hear His gentle voice, we might mistake it for our own thoughts or feelings. But I think God's Spirit speaks to us more than we realize. We just aren't hearing the messages.

God's Spirit also speaks to us through the words of the Bible as well as the words of other people—like a youth leader or a parent or a Christian friend. So it's important that we read our Bibles, make time for our daily devotions, attend church or youth group, and keep alert for the Spirit's voice throughout our day.

When you do hear the Spirit's voice, listen. Take the time to be quiet—without checking your phone or watching TV or trying to multitask. Yes, it's totally hard to do this—*and* it's so totally worth it! Listen to the Spirit's voice in your own spirit. Hear what He tells you as you read the pages of your Bible. And then act on whatever He tells you.

. . . . . . . . . . . . . . . . . . . . . . . . . . .

## God's Spirit Represents Christ

When I was a junior in college, I joined a group called the Ambassadors. Dressed in our blue blazers, we represented our college at community events. When I signed up to join the group, I never imagined that one day I would end up at the exclusive Breakers Hotel in posh Palm Beach, Florida for an international gala...and be able to greet none other than the Princess of Wales. (You've heard of Princess Diana, right? It would be like greeting Kate Middleton today. How amazing would that be?)

I was one of the student volunteers asked to help manage the guests at the gala event. So in a borrowed evening gown, I arrived with my starstruck friends. My job was to stand at the front door, welcome guests, and direct them to the proper dining room.

I knew this job was important because of the way our advisor coached us (okay, threatened us!). We were told that our actions would directly reflect upon the university. We were supposed to represent our college well. I also figured out how big a deal this was when security cordoned off the entryway—and the paparazzi crowded behind my partner, Jamie, and me.

As the guests arrived, a hush fell over the lobby. There she was. The princess.

Jamie and I didn't speak as Princess Diana sauntered past in her dazzling fuchsia gown. We gawked in awe as security whisked her to her seat.

As incredible as the experience was, I made sure to remember that I represented my university. Even if I wanted to scream, "Diana, I love you! Can I borrow your dress?" I didn't. I was a representative of something other than myself.

The Holy Spirit is God's representative. He mirrors God's truth. That means if you sense the Spirit leading your thoughts or guiding your actions, His guidance will always line up with the truth of God's Word. The Spirit *never* leads us in ways that contradict what the Bible says, so when thoughts come into our minds, we need to see if they line up with the truth of Scripture. If they don't, we shouldn't let them into our thought closets. We don't want them taking up valuable space on the shelf.

### God's Spirit Is Our Teacher

My husband is a college professor, and every time he leaves for work, he grabs his briefcase and playfully announces, "Going to stamp out some ignorance!"

That's what good teachers do. They enlighten and instruct. They replace ignorance with knowledge.

God's Spirit does the same thing in our lives. He stamps out ignorance, replacing it with wisdom and knowledge and understanding that are way beyond what we could get on our own even if we studied with the best teachers and aced all of our exams. The Spirit is a Mentor. He teaches and guides with greater understanding than we have on our own. We need mentors.

Imagine how incredible it would be to take music lessons from Beethoven or a physics class from Newton or Einstein. Or to study creative writing with your favorite author. That would be the best, wouldn't it?

When you allow God's Spirit to teach you, you are being mentored by none other than the God of eternity! Amazing! As a Master Teacher, He brings light wherever our understanding is dark. That's really helpful when it comes to wrong thinking. He'll show you how to recognize wrong thinking for what it is— ideas that aren't true or helpful or encouraging—and give you the truth you need.

Before I ever owned an audio version of the Bible, I was still able to recall much of its truth. Of course, I read Bible stories as a child and listened to countless sermons. But honestly, at that age, I was barely able to remember my own phone number. So how would I possibly remember much Scripture as my eyesight began to fail me?

I'm totally convinced that God's Spirit was my Teacher. And because of this, I truly *know* that the Holy Spirit does teach us. I'm so grateful for the role He plays in our lives. Really, learning from Him is the only way to effectively deal with the issues that threaten to crowd our thought closets. We need a Teacher who stamps out the ignorance that can shape our thoughts and feelings. We need a Mentor who will give us wisdom that's way beyond what we could ever get on our own.

### God's Spirit Reminds Us of Truth

One time when I was flying on an airplane, I found myself sitting in front of a little girl and her daddy. We had been sitting on the tarmac for 45 minutes when a voice announced, "Folks, this is your captain. We appreciate your patience. Maintenance assures me that we should be ready to roll in about 15 minutes."

*Fifteen minutes?* At that point, it might as well have been 15 hours. We were long past ready to go! Fellow passengers moaned and groaned as well. And I started making a mental list of all the things I disliked about this airline. I was pulling some ugly words out of my thought closet, for sure!

*We'll just see,* I thought. *It'll be a miracle if this plane takes off in 15 minutes.*

But I really wasn't looking for miracles in that moment. I was grabbing things out of some dark corner of my thought closet, things that were ugly, ill-fitting, and making me tense. My negative thoughts were suddenly interrupted by the voice of the little girl in the seat behind me.

"Daddy," she said, "I spy something blue."

Determined to be cheerful, the father began to guess, "Is it that bug?" And so the game went.

"Daddy, I spy something *good*," she said.

Her dad laughed—probably for the same reason I did when she said that. It was pretty hard to spy anything good right now.

"Is it a bag of M&Ms?" he asked.

"No," his daughter chimed.

"Is it your new shoes or your sweet smile?"

A tenderness washed over me as I eavesdropped on their exchange. Their words cut through my complaining and frustration and reminded me to fix my thoughts on "something good."

In that moment I thought of Philippians 4:8: "Whatever is true, whatever is honorable, whatever is right, whatever is pure, whatever is lovely, whatever is of good repute, if there is any excellence and if anything worthy of praise, dwell on these things" (NASB).

After I remembered that verse, I was able to change my thinking. Instead of complaining, I was able to think of things that were true and good and "worthy of praise." *I spy something lovely, Father*, I began to pray. *You have provided opportunities for me to experience. You have opened doors and made my paths straight.* I reminded myself that delays and inconveniences were just some of the bumps along the road.

Once I began to fix my eyes on things that were true and good, I was able to enjoy the rest of my journey. When I chose to put "praiseworthy" thoughts in my thought closet, I stopped being irritated and annoyed with the airline. Suddenly waiting an extra 15 minutes wasn't a big deal—even if everyone around me was saying that it was.

# I Spy

Let's play a game of "I Spy." But not just any old version. Let's play the "something good" version. Set a timer for one or two minutes and, as fast as you can, write down everything good you can "spy." Look around your house and write down things you can see (your dog, your favorite breakfast cereal, your new shoes) as well as things you can't see (the warmth of the sunshine, your baby sister's laughter, the happiness of knowing God). This is a great game to play every week or so. It really helps you tune in to God and the many blessings He's given you!

Who led me to that truth? Was it the sweet little girl and her daddy? Really, it was God's Spirit. One of His roles is to lead us into all truth. When I was guiding my own thoughts, I was headed down a path that was making me more upset and annoyed and bitter—a path further and further from truth and goodness and joy. Not somewhere I wanted to go!

When I'm dealing with issues, when I'm stressed and overwhelmed, I need a better guide for my thoughts and emotions. I need God's Spirit to lead me to truth. When I try to lead myself, I don't always end up at the right place.

If we make the decision to follow the guidance of God's Spirit, we trade our grumpy and unhelpful thoughts for thoughts that are uplifting and helpful. That's because God understands best what we need to keep in our thought closets and what we need to toss.

## Listen

When it seems like life is getting crazy out of control and one thing after another is going wrong, it might seem like you need to do more and more to keep up. But that's when you actually need to stop and slow down and listen. Listen for what God is trying to tell you. Listen to His wonderful words of encouragement and advice and love. Because that's going to help you when nothing else does.

Sure, you can give yourself some positive self-talk. You can tell yourself to cheer up, to walk on the sunny side of the street, to whistle while you work, or to grin and bear it. You can tell yourself that your problems aren't really that big a deal and that you're actually doing just fine. But none of that is going to solve anything. It might make you feel better in the moment, sure. But it's not going to help in the long run.

When you take the time to fill your mind with God's thoughts—those words that are true and beautiful and life-giving—you'll always have those words stored in your closet, ready to reach for when you're having a tough day. Or a tough week. Or a tough year even. When you're having trouble with school or friends or family. When you're just feeling down for no particular reason at all. When your emotions are overwhelming.

If God's truth is stored in your thought closet, you'll find it much easier to hear the voice of the Holy Spirit when He speaks to you. And when you hear His voice, you can follow His lead and grow in faith and understanding as you become the girl He's designed you to become.

The truth will always lead you straight to Jesus. All you need to do is tune in to His voice.

## *THINGS TO THINK ABOUT*

- What are the biggest, most important things filling up your thought closet? What are some of the things you're worried about or stressed about right now?

- Are you reaching mainly for your own words or God's words as you try to figure out what to do? Why?

- What can you do to better tune in to the Holy Spirit and hear His voice?

- What have you learned about the Holy Spirit in this chapter? What do you think He might be trying to teach you?

## Part 2

# SEVEN MUST-HAVE
# PIECES FOR
# YOUR THOUGHT CLOSET

How's your thought closet looking so far? Still a little bit messy with piles of stuff everywhere? That's completely understandable! Anytime you do a major cleaning, the workspace is probably going to look worse before it looks better. That's just part of the process.

We *have* come a long way, though. We've talked about the danger of listening to—and believing—lies and negative words. We've realized the importance of playing the keep-or-toss game when it comes to our words, thoughts, and comments. We've dealt with the danger of wrong assumptions and learned to accept our imperfections and perhaps even embrace them. And we've learned that when everything seems to be falling apart, the best thing to do is to tune in and listen to God.

We've also begun the process of filling our thought closets with truth and perhaps rearranging some of the good we uncovered. First the clean-out had to be accomplished. Now we're going to start putting things into your thought closet—including seven must-have pieces. These always-flattering items will never go out of style, and they'll be the first things you reach for when you're searching for the perfect words to clothe yourself in. So don't just shove them in a basket or a corner of your closet. Instead, put them right where you'll see them when you open the closet door. They're that necessary!

These seven must-have pieces come straight from the Bible. The poetical books of Psalms and Proverbs speak to us personally and from the heart. That's why we need to use their words when we talk to ourselves.

In these final seven chapters, we're going to page through some passages from those books of truth so we can fill our thought closets with their amazing words.

Each of these passages will fill your soul with truth and joy while helping you discover how to stock your mind and your heart with truth about the goodness of God.

Before we jump in, let's pray this verse together: "Beloved, I pray that in all respects you may prosper and be in good health, just as your soul prospers" (3 John 2 NASB).

Okay, let's get going. We have some fun shopping to do!

# 5

## *PIECE #1*
# DAILY MAINTENANCE

*Ick! What is that smell?* Sarah wondered. She sniffed in her brother's room. Nope, not coming from there—which was actually a surprise. Bathroom? Nope. Utility room? Yep—that's where the smell was strongest. And the source? The cat's litter box.

Oops. It was Sarah's job to scoop the kitty litter every day. And it had been at least a few days—probably more like a week—since she had. When she looked closer, she noticed that litter had spilled everywhere, the box was filled with you know what, and she'd probably have to take it outside, dump the litter in the trash, and scrub down the entire box. #gross

She knew she could have avoided the extra work if she'd been scooping it out every day. Usually, Sarah was pretty tidy about stuff—well, some of it. She was basically obsessed with keeping her desk and all the apps on her phone organized. But when she didn't like a job, she had no trouble letting it slip. Like now. With the nasty cat litter box. The *very* nasty cat litter box.

No wonder her mom kept bugging her to do her chores daily. A job that would have taken just a few minutes was now going to take way too long—and it was Sarah's own fault.

• • •

Like Sarah, doing your chores and keeping stuff clean is probably *not* the thing you look forward to most in your life. But there's a reason for a daily cleaning routine and a lesson to be learned from the litter box: Keeping something clean is easier when you tend to it daily.

Something like a cat litter box. Or a school backpack. Or a bathroom counter. Or a thought closet.

When we receive new life from God, He declares that "the old life is gone; a new life has begun!" (2 Corinthians 5:17 NLT). Neglecting our new, clean selves—like neglecting our chores—allows dirt and grime to collect on the surface of our souls. That nasty stuff works itself down deep into our hearts, and it definitely dulls our shine. To stop this from happening, we need to pay attention.

That's where talking to ourselves comes in. We must tell ourselves to tune in to the right kind of talk.

After we've cleaned out our thought closets—you know, with that game of keep-or-toss—we need to *keep* them clean. And that means daily maintenance, paying attention to what we put in them and guarding the door to keep any junk from entering. Ideally, we want to spend some time every day keeping our thought closets clean.

Doing this takes practice—and remembering. It's a habit we need to form, like brushing our teeth or taking our vitamins or applying our acne medication. When we do those things, we stay healthy and clear up problem areas. Once we've been doing these things over and over and over, they become habits. *Good* habits. And that's what we're looking to do with the maintenance of our thought closets. We want to develop good habits of keeping in the good and keeping out the bad.

When we wipe away the dirt from our lives by spending time

with God every day and telling Him our worries, problems, and concerns, we dress ourselves in our best. We look good, we feel good, and we don't have to attack a big cleanup job, because we've been practicing our daily thought-closet habits.

## Wake Up!

Have you ever fallen asleep in the middle of something—like a movie or even a class—and awakened to wonder where you were and what was going on? When you drifted off, you missed some important stuff in the movie or your teacher's lecture, and you had no clue what was happening.

It's kind of the same way in our lives and in our minds. If we aren't taking the time to put good stuff into our hearts and minds, we can become sleepy and apathetic about some of our poor choices and negative attitudes. Instead of keeping our eyes open and paying close attention to what we're allowing into our minds, we neglect the daily habit of filling our thought closets with good and true thoughts. We slowly get used to the grimy buildup of junk—negative words, confidence-destroying thoughts, messages that simply aren't true—that makes the surface of our souls icky and dirty. Worse, we begin to fool ourselves that everything is just fine the way it is.

Now, I'm not talking about the waking up the way we do after a night's sleep. You know, when you sit up, open your eyes, and come out of dreamland. This is a different kind of waking up. I like to describe it as "becoming undeceived."

Let me explain. *Undeception* happens in that moment when you suddenly get it. When something that made no sense at all suddenly makes sense. When a hazy sky gives way to a clear one. When darkness is replaced by light. It's like when a character in a book or movie suddenly sees something for what it is. They understand. They get it. And the story changes from that point on.

Our own undeceptions are the changing points of our stories as well. The initial undeception that leads us to faith in God is the big one, but other, daily undeceptions keep our souls clean and sparkling and shiny.

At these moments, we are most alive and awake and alert. We see things clearly. We're able to make good decisions. We're able to focus on what matters most to us. And we want to be like this all the time, right? That's why we need to fill our thought closets with the results of these undeceptions. We need constant reminders of what is true and good and real in our lives. And so we need to develop the habit of constantly challenging ourselves to be totally aware, awake, and tuned in. No dozing off in class! If we do doze off, we're in danger of having no clue what's going on.

## Completely Distracted

Have you ever been so immersed in something—a good book, your phone, a Netflix binge—that you've totally tuned out everything going on around you? When you're completely distracted, you're clueless about the conversations happening around you—maybe even when someone's talking directly to you—and are completely focused on that one thing. Maybe you don't mean to, but you're sending the message that the one thing you're doing is the most important thing in your world right then. It's the thing you're treasuring the most.

Now, think for a moment about some of the main distractions you have in your life. And really think about this because distractions come in many packages. Selfish indulgences distract us. So do annoying problems. And sometimes something that's actually pretty minor can pull our attention away from what's really, truly important. Only you know what distracts you and keeps you from making the most meaningful things in your life first in your life.

And let's get real here. Sometimes we don't clearly see what's going on until we spend a moment quietly focusing. That's why it's important to step back from your life—which can be really hard to do!—and try to get some perspective on how you're spending your time and where you're focusing your thoughts. So go ahead and take a minute to step back and try to figure out your top distractions. Try for your top ten. Write them down. Think about them. And pray about them. I'll share some common distractions in a minute.

## *Your Top Ten Distractions*

What's been distracting you lately? Make a list of the top ten things that have distracted you this week:

1.

2.

3.

4.

5.

6.

7.

8.

9.

10.

Looking back at the list, would you consider these major or minor distractions? What do you find helpful about identifying them? What are some better things you could focus on instead?

. . . . . . . . . . . . . . . . . . . . . . . . . . . .

Okay. Here, as promised, are five distractions.

*Distraction 1: your phone.* In the moment, checking your social media feed, responding to text messages, and keeping up with your favorite bloggers and YouTubers can seem like I-have-to-do-this-right-now tasks, but they really aren't urgent at all—unless you need to text your mom back right away! In reality, you could wait to check your Instagram feed until tomorrow or even next week, and nothing in your life would really change. Yet our phones frequently divert our attention and distract us from spending time with our families or doing things in person with our friends or even chatting with God. Yes, our phones can keep us connected with others, but it's better to be connected with real life.

*Distraction 2: pleasure.* Whatever you love to do when you're just hanging out is one of your pleasures. Maybe it's watching your favorite movies or shows. Or listening to music. For me, it's doing nothing but reading (or actually, listening to) books. I so love to sit with a cup of coffee and a few pieces of choice dark chocolate and listen to a good book. That is sheer pleasure for me, and nothing is wrong with pleasure. It's necessary for a healthy soul. But balance—between church activities, home-work, working out, extracurricular commitments, a part-time job, and pleasure—is also necessary.

*Distraction 3: the opinions of others.* What people think of me—or what I *think* they might be thinking of me—can cause so much internal static that I'm unable to tune in to the truth. Besides, it's way too easy to misread text messages or social media comments and assume somebody meant something that she really didn't mean at all. That's where staying awake and alert helps. When you're tuned in to the truth, you're not as easily influenced by the opinions someone may or may not be forming about you. And even if your hunch is right, you'll have put yourself in a place of confidence and contentment so that their opinion just won't matter very much.

*Distraction 4: fear of failure.* I admit it. I'm a type-A perfectionist clear through to the bone. I'm constantly distracted by the desire to do things perfectly—or not do them at all. But not everything has to be done perfectly all the time. (I can't believe I'm saying this!) There is such a thing as *good enough* at certain times and in some areas of life. Studying too much and not sleeping enough isn't healthy. Your clothes and makeup don't always have to be on point. Your friends will still like you even if you don't respond to their messages right away. Chilling out isn't the same as giving up.

*Distraction 5: avoidance of conflict.* You shouldn't try to cause drama, but totally avoiding all conflict can keep you from approaching life in a healthy way. If there is a problem that needs to be solved—a conflict with a teacher about a seemingly unfair grade, an important thing you need to discuss with your volleyball coach, a friendship issue that's really been bothering you—you need to deal with it. This distraction can really get under your skin and totally drain your energy. It can also keep you from filling the closet of your mind with thoughts, words, and comments that are positive, healthy, and true.

Okay, those five distractions are on many of our lists. Do any of these distract you? I'm guessing at least one of them does.

Now, did you notice that not one of the five distractions is illegal, immoral, or unethical? None of them are necessarily *bad*. They are all decent or even good things. They just require you to intentionally establish some balance in your life, and that requires deliberate thought.

So don't automatically assume all your distractions are sinful and wrong—because they're not! In fact, most—if not all—of them probably aren't. But when we allow life's distractions to keep us from pursuing our treasures—from investing in the most important things in our lives—those "harmless" distractions can become stumbling blocks for us.

So what about your distraction list? What's keeping you from putting your time and energy into the real treasures of your life?

And what exactly do we mean by *real* treasures? To help you think about this, I'll share with you some of mine.

*My faith.* I may say I need this or that in a given period of my life, but what I truly need in every period of my life is a relationship with God. I treasure the closeness and amazing friendship I can have with Him through prayer, reading the Bible, and going through a devotional book.

*A sense of purpose.* I highly value the feeling that I'm spending my time and energy on something that has meaning, something that will last.

*My family.* I don't ever want to neglect my relationships with my family because of something that might seem more important at the time.

*Self-discipline.* This virtue has been important to me since I was a teen. I realized long ago that if I'm not self-disciplined, I'm totally affected by the whims and emotions of every circumstance. I'm like a leaf in the wind, skittering this way and that with every random gust.

*God's approval.* I don't want just a relationship with God; I want Him to be pleased with me. I want to sense His pleasure in the way I interact with people through the hours of my day.

## *My Treasures*

· · · · · · · · · · · · · · · · · · · · · · · · · · ·

What are the treasures in your life—the things that are truly meaningful, the things that you cherish the most? Write them down here:

Every now and then—especially when you're feeling distracted—take time to look back at this list so you can once again focus on what truly matters.

· · · · · · · · · · · · · · · · · · · · · · · · · · ·

So how about *your* material treasures? Be thinking about what they might be as we take a peek into another closet.

## Treasures

When my friend Karen went to the Louvre Museum in Paris, she passed through gallery after gallery of famous paintings. She saw masterpiece after masterpiece, each one inviting her to linger and look at it even as the next one beckoned.

Eventually she wandered into a larger room that had only a few paintings at one end and even fewer along the sides. She told me how the crowd had gravitated to a lone portrait on the farthest wall. An entire wall for one painting? It might seem a little strange, but Leonardo da Vinci's *Mona Lisa* is worthy of such prominence.

What Karen saw in that room supports what the Bible says: "Wherever your treasure is, there the desires of your heart will also be" (Matthew 6:21 NLT). Like the *Mona Lisa*, treasures catch our attention. Treasures capture our interest. Treasures draw us in.

That's true about our thoughts too. We think most about what we treasure.

Just as the directors of the Louvre do, we display our treasures in prominent positions on the shelves of our thought closets. Those truly valuable things should have walls of their own because they are our top priorities. I like to think of them as resting on the shelves just inside the door where they're easy to spot and easy to grab when we need them.

If you came into my bedroom and opened my closet door, the first things you would see would be the red Coach bag my sister-in-law, Carrie, gave me for my birthday alongside the backpack Karen brought me from her trip to Paris. Every time I open the door of the closet, my treasured bags are right there.

Our thought closets should be the same way. Every time we open our thought closets to get something out, our treasures—what we prioritize as most important to us—should be the first things we see.

But if our treasures are so valuable, why do they sometimes get shoved to the back? That's simply the nature of distractions. They take up more space in our thought closets than we can really afford to give them. As a result, our greatest treasures may be shoved up against the back wall, nearly inaccessible and basically invisible.

So how do you keep your treasures front and center?

You do that by talking to yourself. By talking to your soul.

What you tell your soul at important decision points throughout your day is key. When your soul is tuned in, alert and awake, your closet will stay sparkling clean and organized. Here's what I mean.

Whenever I'm asked to do something, I first ask myself, *How does this fit into my life purpose?* The request might be speaking to a group or volunteering somewhere or doing something else that's a good thing. If I don't have a good reason for saying *yes* to the opportunity, I won't accept the offer. The invitation may have been an amazing opportunity. (And believe me, when the offer involves a beach, it's awfully tempting!) But even good things can become distractions if they shove our treasures to the back of the closet.

Now, this doesn't mean you need to overanalyze every little decision. But the two questions to ask yourself in any situation are these:

*Does this allow me to protect my treasure?*
*Does this cause me to neglect my treasure?*

If we keep our thought closets clean and organized, answering those questions will usually be pretty easy for us. And keeping the light on in the closet helps too! It's impossible to find anything when you're groping around in the dark.

That's why you really need to pay close attention to your treasures and take note of what distracts you from them. And those distractions aren't always going to be things that are obviously negative or sinful. Even good things can sometimes distract us from what is best.

## The Problem with Distractions

Imagine that over summer vacation, you and your mom did a big redo of your room. You painted the walls, sold a bunch of your outgrown clothes, childhood toys, and little-girl furniture at a yard sale, and bought some new trendy furniture and decorations that fit your new style and stage of life. Together, you sewed some curtains, made some pillows, put together a photo collage, and tied everything together in a theme that featured your favorite colors and designs. Now your room is Pinterest worthy, and it looks like it's straight out of a decorating magazine—and you love it! For the first time in history, you actually feel like keeping it clean and organized.

This is a good thing, right? After all, hasn't your mom *forever* been nagging you to keep your room clean? And isn't it nice to go to sleep in a cozy, picture-perfect room, knowing that you can find exactly what you need the next morning?

But now imagine that you allow your legitimate desire for a gorgeous and clean room to gradually take over. When your friend comes over to hang out and do homework after school, you scold her for not taking her shoes off. When your sister comes in to play a game, you don't let her sit on your white rug because you're afraid she'll get it dirty. When your brother comes up with some popcorn and wants to hang out and talk, you demand that he eats the popcorn first before he even enters your room. You're obsessed with keeping your room perfect.

Here's where the problem comes in. You tell yourself that you're making it a priority to have a clean room, be organized, and keep things looking nice. But your room is distracting you from the real treasures—your family and friends. Your obsession with having a perfect room has pushed the real treasure into the back corner of your closet.

So how can you keep this from happening? By telling yourself to wake up, pay attention, and focus on your true treasures. Doing so will help you put those distractions firmly in their place.

## Roaring Lion

In 1 Peter 5:8, Satan—the enemy of our souls and the one responsible for our lying, untrue, and destructive thoughts—is compared to a roaring lion: "Stay alert! Watch out for your great enemy, the devil. He prowls around like a roaring lion, looking for someone to devour" (NLT).

That passage has always totally confused me. How does a roaring lion sneak up on anyone? Unless you happen to be deaf, you can't help but notice his approach. His roar gives him away, even if you're busy with other things. You'd for sure notice it, wouldn't you?

That question sounds logical, but what if we heard that roar all the time? What if we heard it so often that we gradually tuned it out and actually became desensitized to it? It would be like living in a house next to the railroad tracks. After a while, you don't even hear the trains. Similarly, we can become so used to the distractions all around us that we barely notice their influence.

And that's where the problem starts.

Remember my telling you that I would become so frustrated with myself and call myself an idiot all the time? Even though I'd replaced that lie with the truth in my thought closet, it still popped up from time to time.

What's going on? Why does that happen?

The lion that prowls outside the door of my thought closet is making a racket. He is snarling lies and growling insults at me. If I—even just once—agree with that hateful label of "idiot" during the day, it once again becomes mine. That nasty word goes right back on the shelf of the closet until I once again get it out of my closet.

Until I let that thought in, though, it's not my thought. It belongs to the enemy. I don't want anything he has to give, and I know you don't either.

Satan tries to fill our thought closets with negativity and untruth—one word at a time, one thought at a time. But those thoughts aren't yours unless you make them yours. *I'm not good*

*enough...I can't do anything right...I'm just going to give up*—
those thoughts aren't yours unless you embrace them and invite
them into your thought closet. If you do that, you'll find yourself grabbing them out of your closet again and again. But when
you're awake and alert, you'll recognize them and say, "Hey!
There's no room for you in here."

Choosing the thoughts to put in your closet is like shopping for clothes. As I've asked you before, you wouldn't go to
the local garbage dump, pick through the trash, and then pull
out a stained, smelly, and torn pair of jeans to wear, would you?
Of course not! Now, at the other extreme, imagine that money
were no object. Where would you choose to go shopping? (I'd
hit Nordstrom, Saks, and Rodeo Drive!) Wherever you chose to
shop, you'd pick out only the finest, best fitting, most flattering
clothes money can buy, wouldn't you?

Why? Because you intend to wear them.

Now, apply that idea to your thought closet. You'll clothe
yourself in whatever you put in there, so shop carefully. Don't
just throw something in the closet because you constantly hear
it. *Loser. Idiot. Airhead. Worthless*—refuse to let these thoughts
enter. Those nasty, dirty pieces don't come from within you, so
don't let them in!

Let the lion roar outside the door all he wants. The more con-
sistently you refuse to embrace what he tells you, the sooner he'll
take his Dumpster designs elsewhere. And the cleaner and more
beautiful your thought closet will be.

So be aware of the real enemy. Be alert for his tactics and
keep your soul tuned in. Remind yourself that the One who lives
within you is greater than the one who roars at the door!

If you have to be obsessive about something, be obsessive about
the desire to guard your treasures and speak truth to your soul.

And remember, it's easier to keep something clean and organized if you maintain it every day. So remind yourself to make

cleaning out your thought closet a daily habit. You can even write it down on your to-do list or in your planner! That kind of daily maintenance will prevent your having to do a major cleanup down the road. Oh girl, keeping something clean is always, always easier when you tend to it daily.

## THINGS TO THINK ABOUT

- What are some things you forget to maintain daily? What is the result when these things get out of control?

- Develop a plan for dealing with your top ten distractions. What will you do to shift your attention to the real treasures in your life—and keep it there?

- What pieces do you want front and center in your thought closet? What steps will you take to keep them there and to prevent them from getting shoved to the back corner?

## PIECE #2
# HOPE

"Mom, I have no idea what to do! Can I just say I'm sick and come home? Please? Nobody will ever know!"

Caitlyn frowned and tried to keep a good attitude as she listened to her mom say exactly what she did not want to hear. Something about honoring your commitments and building character and doing the right thing. *Not* what she was wanting to hear right now.

When Caitlyn and her best friend, Taylor, had gone through the training to be junior counselors at their church's summer camp, everything had sounded like so much fun. Living in a cabin all summer. Hiking and swimming and boating and horseback riding. Teaching elementary school kids about God and being a role model they could look up to. Caitlyn and Taylor had spent so many fantastic summers as campers, and they were totally pumped to give back and become counselors themselves.

Except…

Even though Caitlyn and Taylor had talked about it in training and had role-played numerous situations, Caitlyn didn't realize how helpless she would feel when a camper was overwhelmed with homesickness. Or when a camper refused to listen. Or when a camper was being downright mean and bullying another girl in the cabin. Sure, she had help from the senior counselors and staff—who were awesome, by the way—but she'd had no idea how hard this junior counselor job would actually be. All she wanted to do was run away and go home. She was so done with this!

• • •

Have you ever felt like Caitlyn—wanting to just run away when things got difficult? To just leave a situation behind and let someone else pick up the pieces or fix the mess that you simply don't want to deal with?

It's easy to imagine ourselves as totally capable. We're prepared and ready and confident. We've *got* this!

And then…something happens. Or a whole bunch of somethings happen. And suddenly we're feeling shaky and not so confident and we just want to escape. Know what I mean? Yep, of course you do.

*The Princess and the Goblin* by George MacDonald is one of my favorite stories. (What girl doesn't love a good princess story?) At one point in the tale, the young Princess Irene allows fear to overcome her, and she foolishly chooses to run away from the safety of her castle out into the dark mountains. MacDonald writes, "But that is the way fear serves us: it always sides with the thing we are afraid of."

That's why we can never side with fear, because fear is never on our side. That's why Caitlyn's mom refused to side with her daughter's fear. She knew that allowing Caitlyn to run away from her responsibility at camp wouldn't help her at all. She knew Caitlyn had to face her fear so it wouldn't enslave her. Caitlyn's mom also knew that dealing with the situations at camp would help make Caitlyn stronger when she faced other difficult situations in her life.

Caitlyn's mom wanted her to walk through the experience so she could know hope—rooted in her knowledge of God—instead of running from what was hard—following fear and leaving camp. Hope that by God's grace, things would go well at camp. Hope that in God's strength, Caitlyn could deal with situations when things didn't go well. And hope that God would make the camp experience a blessing for campers as well as counselors.

Fear betrays us, but hope in the Lord never does. Fear makes us feel weak, but hope in God gives us confidence.

So rather than giving in to fear and worry, remind yourself to hope in the power and protection God will give you. The God of hope will always be on your side, cheering you on and defending you. Fear always works against you. It deceives you, manipulates you, and eventually messes up your life. In sharp contrast, hope in the Lord shows you what is true, points you in the right direction, and puts you on a path for your good and His glory. When you have placed your hope in God, you feel better physically, mentally, emotionally, and spiritually. Hope in the God of all hope is something steady to hold on to when fear and worry rock your world.

Clearly, the best way to have hope is to look to God and then to look outside yourself, to turn your gaze to the other people in your life. Caitlyn needed to focus not on her own insecurities about being a good and effective camp counselor but instead on the needs of her campers. Who needed a hug? Who needed to hang out and talk about Jesus? Who needed a gentle reminder to treat other people the way they want to be treated? Caitlyn needed to tell herself to look up to God and then look out at the people around her and touch them with God's love.

## Downcast

When you're frustrated about a situation, you don't usually describe yourself as "downcast," do you? You probably use words like "sad," "bummed," "disappointed," or even just "ugh." But "downcast" kind of makes sense. It's easy to get an image of a downcast person—her head is hanging down, her mouth is turned down, and she's kind of dragging herself along.

Now, it's super normal to feel downcast from time to time. Ever since Adam and Eve sinned in the Garden of Eden, sadness has just been part of the human lot in life.

When one of the psalmists was feeling rock-bottom downcast, he opened his personal journal, and we can peek at its tearstained pages.

> Why are you downcast, O my soul?
> Why so disturbed within me? (Psalm 42:5).

I used to think this writer was giving himself a lecture. *Now, come on, soul! You know better. Act like a believer! You're not supposed to be depressed or downcast. What's wrong with you? You're supposed to have hope. Better pull it together!*

But now I see something different in these words. After all, everyone feels depressed at times. Even super happy people sometimes feel sad. Even Christians—who have every reason to feel hope—sometimes experience feelings of hopelessness. We wish things could be one way, but our wishes rarely match the way things actually are. That's why it's easy—and very natural—for us to lose hope sometimes.

And that's why I now think this journal entry in the book of Psalms is basically honest self-talk. The writer was searching his soul for the reasons behind his feelings. It was kind of like he was doing an interview with his soul. And he started the interview with a simple question.

*Why? Why are you downcast?* The psalmist opened the door of his thought closet to find out why everything hanging in there was some shade of blue. (I know, blue is a pretty color! But you know—feeling the blues?)

We can learn a few important things from this psalmist's journal entry. First of all, we see that he is *honest*. The writer acknowledged that he felt sad and bummed, and that's the most important first step to take. Figure out what you're feeling and give it a name. Feelings of sadness won't go away just because we ignore them, run from them, drown them out, or deny them. Think about Caitlyn and her gig as a summer camp junior counselor. Running away from the challenges she encountered and going home wouldn't really solve her problem. In fact, it would probably make certain fears worse than ever. That's why it's so essential to identify your feelings and admit to yourself the truth about what you're experiencing. Even if—and maybe especially if—you don't really like those feelings.

The next important thing to discover in the journal entry is that the writer was *perceptive*. The writer realized that something was wrong, and he knew it didn't get that way for no reason at all. So he decided to scrutinize his thought closet.

> Why are you down in the dumps, dear soul?
> Why are you crying the blues? (Psalm 42:5 MSG)

It might seem a little weird—especially if you're not the kind of girl who keeps a journal—but whenever you're feeling that downcast feeling, ask yourself some questions. *Why am I feeling so sad? Why does everything seem so awful and impossible to me? What might be causing me this anxiety and worry?* If you've never done this exercise before, now is a great time to start. Grab your water bottle or pour yourself a glass of lemonade (or hot cocoa if it's cold out!) and maybe even fix a little snack, hang out on your bed or couch, and have a little chat with your soul.

## Table Legs

You have at least one table in your house, right? Tables are useful for a lot of things. You can eat at them, work at them, or pile things on top of them.

While you're having this little interview with your soul, I want you to have a picture of a table in your head. You can even draw a table in your journal if you'd like!

Okay, imagine with me for a moment that you *are* a table. (Stay with me—I have a point!) It doesn't really matter what kind of a table. Just make sure that your table has four legs. Why? Because even if one leg is loose or damaged, the whole table will be shaky. All four legs are needed to keep the table in balance.

That same thing is true with us. When one of the four essential areas of our life is loose, damaged, neglected, or even missing, we will be shaky and imbalanced. We will easily tip toward sadness and fall into despair. Furthermore, a damaged table can't possibly hold any extra weight, so when stress piles up on us, we wobble, we lean, or we collapse. We need four working legs to keep ourselves in balance!

And what are those four legs?

### Leg #1: Your Emotional Well-Being

As a girl in her teens, you're undoubtedly very familiar with emotions—your own as well as those of your friends. Drama is probably no stranger! Our emotions are precious and powerful, and we need to pay attention to them. But we also need to realize their limitations. If you try to think with your feelings, for instance, you might come to all sorts of false conclusions and bad decisions. When we forget to use our minds and look at the facts, our emotions can totally take over, and that's not good. That's when our table gets shaky and could collapse—or at least everything could slide off it.

Emotions are supposed to serve us and strengthen us. Left to themselves, however, emotions can take control of us, and things can spiral out of control when that happens. We can misread other people. We get confused about our own feelings. We can say or do things in the heat of the moment that we'll eventually regret. We can damage friendships and hurt our family members. All because of relying on our emotions instead of the facts about what's true and real. That's why we need a thought closet stocked with timeless truth, or we will clothe ourselves with the feelings of the moment.

When I was a teenager, I was prone to moodiness. (Sound familiar?) But often my moods had nothing to do with the people or the circumstances surrounding me. Instead, they had everything to do with my own emotions. That was pretty much the case whenever I was grumpy, sad, or angry.

Our problems usually have less to do with our circumstances than with the way we choose to *feel* about those circumstances.

Remember, feelings aren't the same thing as facts.

Emotions are very real, but that doesn't mean they always correspond with reality. So of course I'm not suggesting we throw out our feelings and pretend they don't matter. No way! Emotions are important gifts from God. But because they can be very powerful and very present, we can easily believe they represent facts. When that happens, take a moment to have a little interview with yourself.

Ask yourself why you feel the way you do. Acknowledge that your emotions *are* real and that they *do* matter, but they might not be based on facts.

When you discover the real source of your feelings, check to make sure you aren't believing any lies about the situation or issue. Focus on the truth. Invite God to help you, and He will.

## *Fact or Feeling?*

What emotions are you feeling right now? Quickly jot down whatever comes to mind. Make a list here:

Now, go back and look at what you wrote down. Are these emotions based on facts? Take a moment to reflect on what is going on in your life.

You can also ask yourself, *Do I think with my feelings? Do my feelings serve me well, or am I their slave?*

Interviewing yourself—really trying to probe and figure out what's going on—allows you to take an honest look at your emotions so you can compare them with the truth. Then you can tighten up that shaky table leg if you need to.

### Leg #2: Your Physical Health

God created our amazing bodies and made them able to do great things—like run track, dance hip-hop, and play softball—so we need to take care of our physical selves. If you're not feeling well overall, that might be a signal from your body—which has been growing and changing and needs to be taken care of—that you're not meeting its basic needs. Our bodies need adequate rest, healthy food, and good exercise.

As a teenager, you need to make sure you're well rested. That can be a challenge when homework—not to mention texting friends and hanging out on social media and keeping up with extracurricular commitments—makes for late nights. But you need to get some solid, unbroken sleep. And more than four or five hours a night.

You know what happens when you're super tired. You're prone to cry more easily, lose your temper faster, and forget things. We all do! If this leg of your table gets too weak and tired, the whole table feels shaky. So before you assume the worst about any situation, make sure you've had enough rest. You might just be exhausted.

The food we choose to eat matters too. While we shouldn't obsess about food and calories, we do need to make sure we're eating healthy—enough protein, not too much sugar, plenty of water—and that we're aware of any food allergies or intolerances we might have. If gluten or corn makes you feel icky, don't eat those things. If you feel yourself getting irritable and shaky when you skip meals, eat small meals frequently. You know what works for you—or if you don't, talk to your parent or your doctor to figure it out.

We also need to be exercising regularly, whether that's playing tennis or taking dance classes or riding bikes or even just walking around the block. Our bodies are meant to move, and exercising is a great habit to develop right now if you haven't already. Researchers have found that when we exercise, our pituitary glands can release as much as five times as many mood-boosting beta endorphins as they do when we are resting. Simple translation: We feel better when we move!

## *Clues*

. . . . . . . . . . . . . . . . . . . . . . . . . . . . . . .

How well are you taking care of your body?

How many hours of sleep did you get last night?

What have you eaten today?

What kind of exercise have you done this week?

These answers might give you a clue as to why you're feeling the way you are right now—good or bad. Remember, you need to take care of the physical leg of your table!

. . . . . . . . . . . . . . . . . . . . . . . . . . . . .

So look at your sleep, your eating habits, and your exercise. Is this leg giving your table the support it needs? If not, make some changes!

### Leg #3: Your Mental Sharpness

I hope you realize how capable you are of thinking, learning, and gaining understanding about whatever you're interested in. And that truth has nothing to do with your GPA or standardized test scores or the grade you got on your English final. God gave you intelligence, and we all have different kinds of intelligence. Some of us are math whizzes. Some of us can write brilliant stories. And some of us are super talented at reading the emotions of others and understanding what people need.

And developing the intelligence God gave you will help you with school and homework. So read books for fun. Start following the news and paying attention to current events. Learn to do something useful—like cooking a meal or planting a garden or changing the oil. Learning new things is good exercise for your brain, it can be fun, and it helps you become a well-rounded individual. Plus, you might discover something you really love— something you may want to do for a career someday.

Astronomer Maria Mitchell wrote, "We have a hunger of the mind which asks for knowledge of all around us, and the more we gain, the more is our desire, the more we see, the more we are capable of seeing." Feed your curiosity and this leg of your table will be sturdy.

### Leg #4: Your Spiritual Strength

A deep longing resides in us that only God can meet. Neglecting this longing doesn't make it go away. It will only continue to grow, and it can lead to a feeling of sadness in the soul.

We can try to fill this deep longing with all kinds of stuff— with friends, studying, sports, youth group events—but even good stuff can't and won't totally satisfy like God can.

When you aren't connected to God—when this leg of your table isn't secure—the weakness isn't always obvious. This seems to be the invisible leg, but it's really the weight-bearing leg of the table. When we are spiritually off-kilter, the other three legs get wobbly. When our spiritual needs aren't met, we experience the effects physically, emotionally, and mentally. When this one leg is weak, the whole table is unstable.

Your spiritual nature is the part of you that is eternal. It's the part of you that will live forever and that even now desires to connect with the eternal God.

Because we aren't able to reach God on our own, He came to us in Christ so we could know Him. When we choose to trust Him instead of ourselves for the path we walk in life, the friendships we invest in, and the decisions we make, we find deep satisfaction, and that deep longing is fulfilled.

Until you've asked God to meet that longing, you will have

a shaky table. If you're not sure if you truly know God, talk to a parent or a youth leader or a Christian friend about it. Make certain that the most important leg of your table is strong and sturdy.

## Shaky Table

Have you ever gone out to eat—or maybe to get smoothies or coffee—and had to switch tables because the one you first sat down at was so wobbly that your food and drinks were in danger of sliding off? Sometimes we can feel like that wobbly table. One of our legs—physical, emotional, mental, or spiritual—might be loose and wobbly. When you find that happening to you, sweet girl, take care of yourself. Eat some healthy food. Text or get together with a friend. Read a good book. Go for a run. Spend time reading that devotional your friend recommended.

When your table is strong and sturdy, you'll be prepared when challenges come your way. And you'll find yourself making one of two choices. You can tell yourself, *Okay, you might as well get depressed, give up, and lose heart.* Or you can tell yourself, *Hey, you might as well choose to have hope in God! I'm going to focus on the goodness of God and wait for something good to happen here.* That something might not be a change in circumstances. It may be calmer emotions, a change of perspective, or a sense of God's presence with you—and those are good happenings!

When you make the right choice—when you choose hope, when you look to God—you will help yourself, and you will be able to help others too. Do you realize the impact a true, sunny, from-the-heart smile can have on those around you? Smiling can be like pulling open the blinds and letting morning sunlight stream into a person's life.

But I want to say one more thing before we leave this topic of wobbly tables. If you're feeling frustrated or disappointed or just plain upset, don't eat a gallon of ice cream while you sit in bed watching TV all day. That will only make you feel worse about life!

Instead, interview yourself about the four legs of your table. What's going on emotionally? Have you been taking care of yourself physically? Are you mentally clear and sharp? Are you in a deficit when it comes to spending time with God? Do whatever you need to do to make each leg strong—and then tell yourself to choose hope.

Is it really as simple as making a choice? Yes—and no. It's actually as *difficult* as making a choice! But why choose to be negative when you can instead choose hope in God? If you don't choose hope, you'll automatically be choosing despair.

Hope makes you focus on the potential of something bigger, brighter, and better happening. That's what you see when your soul looks up.

## Taking a Fresh Look

When you choose to look outside yourself—when you focus on God and others and basically stop being absorbed in yourself—you can look back at your own life and see situations more clearly. Suddenly things you didn't really notice come into focus. You may see in your problems promising hints of change, or you may realize you've been learning some important life lessons from the tough circumstances.

We lose hope when we focus only on our own problems. But choosing hope widens our view and therefore changes our perspective. You can see the true size and shape of your challenges as well as your difficulties when you look at them from a different angle.

Problems can look awfully big, and they will try to stare you down and force you to despair. But you don't have to let them win.

Instead, let your issues and your frustrations become your friends. Sounds crazy, but it works! Ask yourself, *What is this situation teaching me about my strengths? What can I learn about my weaknesses? How can this problem strengthen me? In what ways am I growing because I'm dealing with this issue?*

The most hopeful people I know are those who place their trust in God. Freed from the need to always be in control, they're able to rest in Him. Life isn't a struggle to avoid problems. They know everything isn't always going to go perfectly, and they're okay with that. With God's help, they can handle every situation! They don't become hopeless, because their hope is in God, not in themselves or in the solutions to their problems. I have hope even in blindness because I choose to always believe in the goodness of God.

It's not a once-for-all-time choice. It's a choice I make over and over, several times each and every day.

The challenges in your life might seem higher than you can see over, deeper than you can crawl beneath, and wider than you can walk around. It's like Caitlyn's situation as a summer camp counselor. Because she'd been through training and had even been a camper for so many years, she thought she was prepared for anything. Bad weather? She'd packed her rain gear. Her allergies? The camp nurse had her medication. Feeling tired? Sometimes the counselors had iced coffee or a Dr. Pepper to wake them up. Homesick kids? She'd been there herself.

But she wasn't ready for some of the other challenges that hit—bullying, disobedience, and a kid who really, really, *really* wanted to go home. How could she deal with this? These problems were way too big for her!

Caitlyn was right—these challenges *were* too big for her to deal with *all by herself.* But the good news is that she didn't—and we don't—have to face challenges alone. Caitlyn's problems weren't going to be solved by her running away *from camp.*

Instead, they were going to be solved by her running *to God*. And to others who could help her know the right words to say, the right things to do, and the right people to ask for help.

So try to have hope in every situation, no matter how impossible the circumstances might seem. Think about the best; don't focus on the worst. As Helen Keller said, "We could never learn to be brave and patient if there were only joy in the world."

Hope whispers when the world shouts. Hope sits with you when you are alone. It is a blanket of comfort when you are afraid. It is the warmth radiating from the flame of truth. It is the foundation upon which your life can securely stand.

Hope will ground you, anchor you, and make you unshakable. And by the way, your thought closet always has room for a little more hope—but there's no place for despair. So even though you might feel like escaping your problems by running away from them, choose to look out, look up, and have hope.

## THINGS TO THINK ABOUT

- How do you typically respond when you're in a really difficult situation? Do you welcome the challenge and tackle it head on? Is your default, *I'm running as far away from this as I can*? Or something else? What do you think prompts or fuels your response?

- When you face a decision, do you tend to consider the facts, or do you think more with your feelings? Give an example. How well did the facts or feelings serve you?

- What can you do to choose hope over fear?

- Write out a promise from God that can help you not lose hope. Here are a few you can look up to consider: Isaiah 40:31; Romans 15:13; 2 Corinthians 12:9; Philippians 4:13,19.

**7**

## PIECE #3
# WATER

I'm sooooo mad!" Rebecca screamed. Her sister had borrowed the camera Rebecca had spent months saving for and then dropped it in the lake. Yes, it was an accident, and yes, her sister was planning to pay her back, but it didn't change the fact that Rebecca was angry. Really angry.

Grabbing her phone, she looked at the text message from her sister again—and it made Rebecca even more furious, which she didn't think was even possible. *How could she? I can't believe she did that!*

Rebecca was beyond mad! She was boiling with rage. And without even thinking about what she was doing, she grabbed her phone and threw it against the wall. Hard. And then watched it drop.

Oops. *Big* oops. Rebecca knew before she even went to retrieve it that she'd done some major damage. Yep. Sure enough, as soon as she bent down to grab the phone, she saw that the screen was shattered. Majorly shattered. And she knew that if she wanted to replace it, she'd be buying it herself. Not that she had any money right now. That had all gone toward the new camera that was sitting in the bottom of a lake somewhere.

*Why can't I control my temper?* Rebecca moaned to herself. *Why do I always explode when things go wrong and make everything so much worse?*

• • •

After the fact, it's usually easy to realize that we should have calmed down and chilled out when we reacted and our reaction went south. Big-time south. Especially when what we're reacting to is something completely out of our control. Red-hot rage and volcano-like eruptions aren't usually our finest moments. But they're important to pay attention to because our reactions clearly reveal the temperature inside our thought closet.

Even if it seems our nature to explode when things go wrong, we can use soul talk—the thoughts, words, and comments we say to ourselves—to keep our inner thermostat at a cool and steady temperature. Or at least a temperature that doesn't threaten to erupt and shatter everything! It *is* possible to fight fire with water. It *is* possible to calm down and chill out.

## Peace in Chaos

One of the Old Testament words for peace is the Hebrew *shalom*. This word—it even sounds peaceful!—is really a prayer that asks God to secure a person's well-being. Saying *shalom* to yourself is like inviting peace into your thought closet. And peace is a much better option than a volcanic explosion!

But experiencing peace of mind and peace in our hearts can be very challenging because most of the time life outside, swirling around us, isn't peaceful at all. Sure, when you're out on a paddleboard in the middle of a quiet lake or hiking in the woods with your family, outward peace is easy to find. But that's not how we usually live. We're usually rushing from class to class. Or going full-speed in our favorite activities. Or frantically trying to clean our room before our friend comes over. (Or maybe not!) Life can feel stressful and overwhelming and...anything but peaceful. Yet our inner world really can be peaceful even as our outer world goes crazy.

So where does peace come from? Jesus clearly revealed its source: "Peace I leave with you; my peace I give you. I do not give to you as the world gives" (John 14:27).

Before we really get into talking about where peace comes from, let's figure out why we even have sparks of anger in our thought closets. We need to figure out the source of our anger.

## Control Freak

Okay, I totally admit it. I'm a control freak. And not just any kind of control freak. A *blind* control freak. Do you realize how difficult that is?

By nature, I'm a planner. I strategize, organize, analyze, and then enjoy watching everything fall into perfect place.

Or not.

A long time ago, I had to get real with myself and admit that I wasn't totally in control. And I never really could be. That's because ultimate control was never mine to begin with.

I didn't lose control when I became blind; I never had it in the first place. If we truly had control over all the events of our lives, we would have been able to choose when we were born, to whom we were born, and where we were born. We would have selected our own names and even our own DNA. And I guarantee you I would have chosen DNA that made me as tall as Julia Roberts rather than as short as Jennifer Rothschild!

Yep, a lot of the stuff in our lives is totally out of our control. But we seem to think and act as if it isn't. And that's why we get angry and upset when we lose control of a situation we feel we had a handle on—or should have had a handle on. We act as though we've lost something, but we never truly had it at all.

The good news here is that not everything is out of our control. God has left a few *very* important parts of our life up to us.

- We have control over our own attitudes.
- We have control over our responses to circumstances.
- We have control over our choice to seek God.
- We have control over our choice to acknowledge that He is God—and we are not!

Yes, in those situations we have the power to choose, but making the right choice can be really hard. When we recognize that God has ultimate control over our lives and over the world, we can choose to trust Him even when we don't understand His ways. That choice to trust His plan, His ways, and His goodness more than we trust our own ideas is a hard choice to make.

Yet acknowledging God's absolute control over everything and trusting in Him to let His goodness and love guide that control has put so much peace in my thought closet. Peace now sits on a shelf that used to hold unhealthy emotions like anger, bitterness, and annoyance—and peace looks so much better on me! The Bible says, "You will keep in perfect peace those whose minds are steadfast, because they trust in you" (Isaiah 26:3).

Our trust in God is totally linked to the peace we receive from God. Peace comes when we loosen our grip and let down our guard before our heavenly Father. Peace comes when we chill out and give in to God. Peace comes when we do as Psalm 46:10 instructs: "Be still, and know that I am God."

The original Hebrew word for *still* in Psalm 46 has to do with a physical position. Imagine letting your body go limp or relaxing the grip of your hand. It's a pretty simple concept that easily transfers to the psalm—we quiet ourselves by acknowledging that He is God and we are not. And the first step toward doing that is accepting that God has ultimate control and we do not.

But sometimes stuff gets in the way of this perfect peace, doesn't it?

### A Negative Mindset

Some things in this life are legitimately hard. There are things we don't like and don't want but have to deal with anyway. Things like a teacher or coach who isn't fair. A difficult family situation—like parents who are divorced or a sibling who's making really bad choices. Former friends who are now being mean to us. We would never voluntarily choose any of these things.

## *Boiling Point*

What robs you of your peace? What situations or circumstances cause you to boil over? Which people in your life tend to push your buttons and make you hit that boiling point with lightning speed? Jot down the things that really bug you and the people who push you to your boiling point.

Now, pray that God will give you His peace in these situations and with these people.

It's easy to assume that our anger comes to the surface and boils over because of these negative things. But the real source of anger isn't a tough situation or a difficult person. It's the way we choose to think about that tough situation or difficult person. That's why it's so important to choose a peaceful mindset when something might make us angry.

For me, blindness isn't the source of my anger. But my *attitude about my blindness* might be! For Rebecca, her lost camera wasn't the source of her anger. But her *attitude about the lost camera* might have been.

So what do you do when you realize the importance of your attitude? What I like to do is consider my blindness—or anything else that might produce anger—as a bridge. Yes, a bridge. A bridge that takes me somewhere and allows for progress and a new direction in my life.

The alternative mindset is to think of it as a wall. Walls block my view. They prevent me from moving forward. Walls are hindrances, keeping me from where I really want to be, and they really make me mad.

The words you tell yourself can build either bridges or walls. Building one requires just as much emotional energy as building the other, so choose wisely! Hint: Choose the positive mindset. Choose to build a bridge.

## Anger over Adversity

*Life isn't fair!* Have you ever heard someone say that? Have you ever said it yourself or thought it? Of course you have!

I'm going to get a little bit tough here. Life *isn't* fair. Someone who doesn't work as hard as you do wins the race. Some girls have perfectly clear skin and straight white teeth! Some families don't seem to have any problems. But here's the deal with your problems: You need to accept them. Don't let them fill you with anger. I know, I know...that sounds simplistic and not too original, but it's the truth.

No one has promised you that life will be fair. It never has been, and it never will be. It is what it is, and it will be what it will be. Accepting that reality isn't the same as approving of your difficult circumstances. It's just being real about reality!

Dear girl, you have a choice about this hard reality. There are two ways you can deal with the unfairness of life. You can get angry. Or you can accept it.

When you choose anger, you can really wear yourself out. And by the time you notice what you're doing, it's often too late to go back and make things better. Like Rebecca throwing her phone against the wall and totally cracking the screen. She can't have a redo of those moments of anger and rage. Neither can you or I. And we can mess up a lot worse than shattering a phone screen.

The best thing to do is to take your tremendous passion about life's injustices (AKA your anger) and use that energy for good for yourself and for others. You often can't change negative situations, but you can change your reaction to them. For me, accepting the adversity of blindness has become a stepping-stone of hope and encouragement for others. And along the way, slipping up behind me on my pathway, I've found an unexpected companion.

Peace.

So ask God to help you embrace what you can't avoid, accept what you don't like, and let your anger for injustices inspire you to do something positive.

## Stubborn Defiance

When you're totally angry and upset, it might seem impossible to ever let go of that anger. But it's not impossible at all. Not with an all-powerful God in your corner and His truth in your closet!

Maybe, then, it's not that you *can't* let go of your anger. Maybe it's actually that you *won't*. #busted

When you're surrounded by negative people—and a lot of teens can be negative, complaining about school and parents and pretty much anything else—it's sometimes hard to imagine that you can choose to go through your day being happy, hopeful, and upbeat. But you can do it—even if it seems impossible!

## Negative/Positive

Write down ten negative statements about your life. They can be anything at all!

1.

2.

3.

4.

5.

6.

7.

8.

9.

10.

Now, rephrase those statements and change the negative to a positive. I'll give you a few examples. Negative statement: *My room is too small.* Positive statement: *My room is cozy and easy to clean.* Negative statement: *Math is too hard.* Positive statement: *I'm learning to work hard and to keep trying even when something doesn't come easily.*

1.

2.

3.

4.

5.

6.

7.

8.

9.

10.

· · · · · · · · · · · · · · · · · · · · · · · · · · · ·

Your attitude is contagious. Happiness is contagious, and so is anger. Someone has said that anger is one letter short of danger. And it is. But danger to whom? For Rebecca, her cell phone was in danger. But again, the consequences of our anger can be a lot worse than that! Other people—often the ones we love the most—can be hurt by our angry words and actions. Victim number one, though, is you! Defiance—an unwillingness to let go of anger—can really and truly hurt you. And it can hurt you both inside and out. It hurts your self-esteem and impacts your relationships with others. It hurts your present and affects your future. And you are far too valuable to live like that.

So if you want to be a peaceful young woman instead of a grumpy girl, take a good look at your attitude. What is your general mindset? Do you tend to have a negative or positive outlook on life? How do you immediately respond to difficult situations—by getting angry or by accepting them?

Choose to keep peace in your thought closet instead of filling it with anger. Peace is a much better look for you!

## Fire

As a blind person, I've started a few fires in my culinary career. The worst one happened one night when I used pot holders to place a dish in the preheated oven. I carefully positioned the pan on the metal rack and closed the door. I then set the pot holder on the counter and went to another room. After a few minutes, I smelled smoke.

I assumed some of the casserole had bubbled over and was now searing itself onto the bottom of the oven. Wrong! When I opened the oven door to inspect, flames leaped out at me. This was no sauce drip. This was an inferno! What had I done?

If you're an observant reader, you noted that I laid the pot holder rather than the pot holders on the counter, right? Yes, I was cooking the other pot holder. And it didn't smell good.

Home alone, I grabbed a bowl, filled it with water, and threw it into the oven. Almost immediately, I realized I should have turned the oven off first! I'd doused the flames, but now there was an awful electrical crackling, and a strange new smell filled the room.

*Oh no,* I thought. *My oven is electric, and I just poured a gallon of water on those live wires!* (Don't ever do that!) Thankfully, I remembered that flour puts out electrical fires. So I threw five pounds of flour into the oven to smother my mess.

Let's just say we ordered pizza for dinner that night.

Fires demand responses, don't they? But not just any response will do. We need to make wise responses—like using flour instead of water to put out a fire in an electric oven—so we can extinguish the flames. And even though Jesus places peace in our thought closets, smoldering embers of anger and bitterness and other negative emotions can remain.

In fact, we're all kind of like my oven inferno. We all have the potential—in the wrong conditions—to explode. We all have the potential to ignite the smoldering embers within us and create a bigger fire.

Before you get too discouraged here, thinking, *Well, guess there's nothing I can do about my anger,* let me reassure you. There *is* something you can do to make sure you keep your volcanic explosions and oven fires to a minimum. You don't have to let the emotions of anger and rage take over your life even when you feel like a hormonal mess. You *can* stay calm and avoid the damage of a blowup.

You do this by—of course—talking to yourself! Another solid bit of soul talk can prevent a major conflagration.

When your anger rises, what you say to yourself will either calm you down or totally ignite you. Those words you speak to yourself will either be like water or like gasoline. Water will quench the flames; gasoline will fuel an inferno.

So what kind of words do you use when you talk to yourself? What do you say to yourself when your emotions are quickly getting out of control and you know an explosion is on the way? Do you speak soothing words of truth to calm yourself down and tell yourself to chill out, or do you stoke the fire with accusations, bitterness, and self-pity?

Take some time to think about this, okay? When that crucial moment arrives—that moment when you feel like flinging your phone across the room or saying stuff to your sister you know you'll instantly regret—how will you react? If you've already thought about your options and perhaps even made a plan, you'll be much more likely to respond well.

So first, what are some things that ignite your anger? Then, what settles you down when you're mad? What do you say to yourself that brings you peace? You might want to make your own list of gasoline words and water words. I listed some of mine These lists can help us monitor and regulate our soul talk.

| *Gasoline Words* | *Water Words* |
|---|---|
| You always… | I understand. |
| You never… | I don't blame you. |
| You should have… | Good try. |
| You ought to… | Way to go. |
| | There's always next time. |
| | I forgive you. |

Gasoline words always, always make things worse. When we're quick to judge, to point out flaws, and to criticize, our words intensify feelings and make emotions escalate. As the Bible says, "a gentle answer turns away wrath, but a harsh word stirs up anger" (Proverbs 15:1).

Look again at your list of gasoline words. Which of these, if any, do you use when you talk to yourself? Think about a time when the thoughts, words, and comments you directed at yourself stirred up your anger and frustration. Lesson learned?

Now think about the words you usually use when you respond to others—like your brother or sister—in a difficult situation. And be honest with yourself! Which list do you tend to pull from? If you're harsh and quick to judge your siblings, you probably use those same gasoline words in your soul talk to yourself. Just as you shouldn't speak those words to others, you shouldn't speak them to yourself. Your soul needs the refreshing water of God's Word and of kind, tender human words.

## H₂O

Think about water for a moment. It's soothing. It's refreshing. It's exactly what you need when you're overheated and tired and exhausted. Water words can have the same effect on you. They soothe the soul and refresh the heart. They settle your extreme emotions, help you see a situation for what it really is, and give you a more accurate perspective.

Water words are full of grace and mercy. They encourage and cleanse. The Bible says, "A man's discretion makes him slow to anger, and it is his glory to overlook a transgression" (Proverbs 19:11 NASB).

Do you speak peaceful water words, both to yourself and to others? Or do you tend to spout gasoline words? Once again, take a little time to think about this. Maybe pray about it and ask God to help you change your reactions and your words.

Now before we move on, there's something else that's important to remember here. Water words aren't always the calm, peaceful, quiet words you might imagine them to be. Nope! Sometimes water words need to be truthful and corrective, and truth can be hard to hear sometimes. But words of truth spoken in love do bring peace.

Scalding hot water sterilizes, and ice-cold water prevents swelling. Neither temperature is pleasant, but they're effective and life-giving in the right circumstances. You might need to use boiling hot water to sterilize silverware. And if you have a sprained ankle, a freezing cold ice bath will prevent swelling. Water words are the same to our souls. They may hurt for a moment, but the result is healing and health.

I've definitely spoken difficult-to-hear corrective water words to my soul before. I remember feeling embarrassed after saying something to a friend that I shouldn't have said. Totally irritated with myself, I was tempted to throw some gasoline into my thought closet. *Jennifer! What were you thinking? You shouldn't have said that. She's your friend! How could you say such a stupid thing? What is she going to think of you now? You are a lousy friend!*

Even if we never say these words aloud, they still have the power—lots of power—to make situations and relationships worse. They'll stoke the fires of discontent, anger, and self-hatred—all emotions that will find their way into our thought closets and take up valuable space.

So what can we do instead? We can sprinkle some healing water in our thought closet. After saying those words to my friend that I shouldn't have said, I needed to tell myself, *Jennifer, Jennifer, you said that because you felt self-conscious or insecure. But you are secure in God—you know that. You don't need to focus on yourself. Focus on Him and on others. Remember how this happened and why. And remember how you feel right now so you won't do it again.*

Corrective water words don't always make us feel good, but they always make situations and relationships better in the long run. Developing this kind of soul talk is a process, but eventually you'll learn to appreciate yourself enough to find the truth and speak it to yourself. That's why it's so important to not run away from water words that point out a part of your life you need to work on. Remember, scalding hot and freezing cold water both have their uses.

And what about gasoline words? Not every *hard* word is a gasoline word, but every *harsh* word is. It can be hard to tell the difference between hard and harsh. The true test is what those words do to the flames within you. If they ignite anger, they're gasoline. If they bring peace, they're water.

The words you speak to yourself—the thoughts you receive, personalize, and dwell on—can either cause anger to ignite or allow peace to prevail. Long story short? You want water words in your thought closet, not gasoline words. So do your best to keep out those gasoline words! They'll only make your thought closet dangerously hot—and you don't want it to catch fire.

## Make the Trade

If you find yourself reacting like Rebecca did—so overcome by your emotions that you tend to blow up and make everything worse—it's time to get control of your reactions before they control you. Remember, a lot of life swirls out of control all around us. Rebecca, for instance, didn't have any control over her lost camera. But her broken phone? Well, avoiding that was totally within her control.

Learn from Rebecca and start right now to trade your raging anger for peace for your soul. The apostle Paul said, "Since we have been justified through faith, we have peace with God through our Lord Jesus Christ, through whom we have gained access by faith into this grace in which we now stand" (Romans 5:1-2).

When you have peace *with* God, you can receive peace *from* God—the peace that Christ brings. When peace becomes the default setting on the thermostat in your thought closet, those little sparks are just that—little. When you speak words of peace, the sparks won't turn into flames.

When your emotions begin to heat up, you can tell your soul to chill out and calm down.

You, my friend, can choose water over fire.

## THINGS TO THINK ABOUT

- What smoldering embers, if any, are in your thought closet? What situations, circumstances, or people tend to fan those embers into flames?

- What gasoline words do you use when you speak to others (like your siblings)? What gasoline words do you use when you speak to yourself?

- What are some helpful water words you can put into your thought closet?

- Do you believe God is in control of your life? Why or why not? Reflect on that question and ask God to fill you with peace.

## PIECE #4
# MEMORY

"Mom! Not *this* picture!" Emma groaned. "I look so dorky!"

"But that was our really fun camping trip," Emma's mom replied.

"Yeah, but I'm covered with mosquito bites. And look at my hair. I don't think I washed it for a week!"

"I know, but we had such a great time kayaking around the lake and hanging out with the cousins. And someday you'll love looking at that photo. It will bring back such good memories, and you'll be able to look back and see how much you've grown and matured since then. Trust me."

Emma sighed. "Well, I don't feel like that right now. But maybe someday. And you can put it in the scrapbook only if we include some equally awkward pictures of Erika and Ethan!"

Emma's mom grinned. "Deal."

The two continued to sort through the stack of pictures, searching for the perfect ones to capture memories of days gone by. And as they worked, Emma felt the tiniest little twinge of what her mom might be feeling, some small feelings of nostalgia and happiness about the time that had passed.

• • •

Looking back at our memories—from scrapbooks packed with family photos to Instagram feeds full of artsy shots of you and your friends—can fill us with all kinds of emotions. Sometimes when we look back, we want to celebrate because we've come so far. At other times our backward glances bring tears of longing, pain, or regret—or just plain embarrassment! Remembering the milestones in our lives also gives us a chance to see how much progress we've made. A look back helps us to see more clearly who we were and who we're becoming. And it can give us an honest, unfiltered look at ourselves.

Something that's fun to do as you're considering who you are and who you're becoming is to make a bucket list. Think about 10 or 20 or even 50 things you'd like to accomplish in the coming years. It can be anything from running a 5K to learning how to bake a cake to skydiving.

## Bucket List

What are ten things you'd love to accomplish in the coming year? List them here:

1.

2.

3.

4.

5.

6.

7.

8.

9.

10.

If you're feeling inspired, pull out a journal or a piece of paper and keep going!

. . . . . . . . . . . . . . . . . . . . . . . . . . .

At one point in my life, I started writing down my bucket list—my list of life goals. One thing on the list was reading everything C.S. Lewis wrote. I began with *Mere Christianity* and then went on to read *Surprised by Joy*. Of course, I read all the Narnia books. Have you? I love them! Then I happened on an unexpected treasure. It was a delightful fantasy novel that Lewis wrote in 1943 called *Out of the Silent Planet*, the first book in his space trilogy. I totally recommend it!

## Another World

Lewis began his tale by introducing the main character, a philologist—someone who studies literary texts and written records—named Elwin Ransom. As he was taking a walking tour of the English countryside, he ran into some shady characters from his university days. After some dinner and conversation, Ransom was terrified to realize he'd been fooled by his former friends. He woke up astonished to find himself in a metal ball soaring through the light-filled heavens, on his way to another world.

When the spacecraft landed on a planet called Malacandra, Ransom was introduced to a new culture and new perspectives. One such perspective celebrated the unique power and significance of remembering. A friendly Malacandran later described his first encounter with Ransom:

> When you and I met, the meeting was over very shortly. It was nothing. Now, it is growing something as we remember it. But still we know very little about it. What it will be when I remember it as I lie down to die; what it makes in me all my days, that is the real meeting. The other is only the beginning of it.

I love that thought! And it's not as alien as you might think.

The real power of any moment happens when you remember it. The experience might have been good or bad, pleasant or painful, exhilarating or embarrassing—but its intensity and meaning grow when we remember and reflect upon it. It becomes clear—like a picture in a scrapbook—when we place it alongside the other pictures we've stowed away in our thought closets.

Remembering things is so important. In order to grow and learn and mature, we need to recall moments and events of all kinds. That's why we need to make ourselves look back and not ignore the awkward photos or the uncomfortable memories.

## Scrapbook of Memories

Think of your memory as a scrapbook—a big, elaborate one filled with page after page of pictures, quotes, thoughts, and stories. The scrapbook of your memory shows who you are and where you came from. If you look carefully, it can also give you hints about where you're going.

When you look through the pages of that scrapbook, you

might feel like laughing or crying or both. Every image, every story, every quote has a memory attached. Some pages you could look at for hours. Some you might feel tempted to skip over. But they're all important. They're all a part of *you*.

When you look back at the memories in the scrapbook of your mind, which ones should you focus on? Which pictures should you highlight, decorate, and spend time making look pretty? What should you tell yourself to remember? Here's my best advice: Tell yourself to look back only to what is profitable— to what is useful or beneficial or valuable for your healing and growth.

But are the most profitable memories only going to be among your best memories? Your fun vacations and your good hair days? Um...sorry! Some will be, but some won't be. But before you start trying to hide those pictures, wanting to leave them out of your scrapbook, let's consider why it's important to include pictures that bring a little pain alongside pictures you love to look at.

## Memories with a Purpose

Some memories are so amazing that you don't need any encouragement to think about them. You recall with pleasure your favorite birthday party, the time you scored first overall in your gymnastics meet, the day you met your best friend. But other memories bring pain, and revisiting them is really, really hard. The day your dog died. The time you fell out of a tree and broke your leg. Those months of school when the mean girls were bullying you.

It makes sense to us, then, that we would hold on to the good memories and let go of the bad ones. But both kinds of memories can actually be profitable if you choose to remember them in the correct way. You do that by *assigning meaning* to them. Now, this isn't exactly easy. It's something you'll get better at with time. But you can start learning how to do this right now, and it will help you for the rest of your life.

Profitable memories are those memories that add to your soul wellness rather than subtract from it. They make you mature and help you grow instead of dragging you down and keeping you stuck in your own immaturity. Profitable memories contribute to your personal depth and understanding. They challenge you to think broadly rather than narrowing your perspective. That's why profitable recollections can either be pleasant or painful. It's not the memory. It's the *purpose* the memory serves in our lives. Really hard times can yield great wisdom.

Think back to a really hard time in your life. If you ever broke a bone and had to have surgery, it might have left a scar. Or being emotionally hurt might have left an invisible scar on your heart. Either way, that scar is there. It never completely goes away. Now, this might sound really crazy, but I hope a tiny bit of your scar will always be visible as an ever-present and helpful reminder.

Whenever you see that scar, whenever you remember how your injury—either physical or emotional—happened, you will be able to tell yourself some important truths: God provides. God enables me to get through tough things. Situations aren't always as bad as they might seem at first…And that's only the beginning of a list of encouraging truths you can tell yourself.

Painful memories are profitable—they have value in our lives—because they remind us of how God cares for us and loves us and comforts us. Painful memories reassure us that we can always, always trust God. If we block out the painful memory of getting hurt, we also block out the joyful memory of being healed.

So if you have some painful memories and a few scars, don't be afraid to put them in your scrapbook and ask God to shine the light of His truth on them. He can make painful memories profitable as He gives them meaning. He will give you "beauty instead of ashes, the oil of gladness instead of mourning, and a garment of praise instead of a spirit of despair" (Isaiah 61:3).

When you assign meaning to a memory, you label it as something profitable, and that memory enriches your life. If you don't assign meaning to a painful memory, it will still stay negative in your mind. For example, if you take the memory of being teased mercilessly by the mean girls and file it away as a bad time, it's not going to add anything good to your life. But you can give that memory a new label. You can remember it as a time when you learned how to reach out to others and react to meanness with kindness. You can acknowledge that you came out of the whole situation a better person who is now able to be a better friend. And now you've given the memory purpose and meaning. You've made it profitable.

Before we move on, I do want to bring up one thing. If you have a memory that's still really bothering you and it seems impossible to deal with or even recall in its entirety, please talk to someone about it. Your mom or dad, your favorite aunt, your mentor at youth group—one of those people will be able to help you figure out a place to put this difficult memory and what meaning you can assign to it.

## Your Story

This is probably no surprise at all, but happy, pleasant memories can contribute so much to your life if you take the time to recall them. These wonderful milestones and memories will add color and joy to your thought closet. They will become more special and more meaningful as you get older. Trust me, someday you'll experience so much joy looking back at past moments with even more depth and understanding. And allowing yourself to look back—keeping in mind how much you've grown and changed and matured—will make your present experiences even better.

Your memories are your history, your story. They show who you are, and they can influence who you hope to become.

Memories—especially hard ones—can be our best friends or our worst enemies. They become our friends when we learn from them and allow them to teach us. But those tough memories turn into enemies when we avoid them or pretend they don't exist.

Our memories can also keep us from repeating our mistakes. They help us not to worry—knowing we've been able to handle a certain situation, knowing that God has been faithful—and they give us greater understanding about life and God.

So what should you remember? Remember whatever is profitable, whether good or bad. Those experiences have purpose and value beyond just the remembering. Ask God to guide you to the good memories and even the hard ones. Ask Him to help you wisely assign meaning to those milestones.

## Picture This

Look through a family scrapbook or a stack of pictures from your childhood. What memories stand out? Write them down here:

What meaning can you draw from these memories? What have these moments taught you? In what ways did you grow because of them?

·  ·  ·  ·  ·  ·  ·  ·  ·  ·  ·  ·  ·  ·  ·  ·  ·  ·  ·  ·  ·  ·  ·  ·  ·  ·  ·  ·

## Don't Forget

Have you ever written a card to a friend who's moving away or signed a yearbook with the phrase "Don't forget me"? There's something significant about asking someone to not forget. I think not forgetting is more than just remembering. I put things on my to-do list or ask my phone to remind me so I'll remember them. But to "not forget" goes a step further. We cross things off our to-do list or planner pages once we've completed them. Study for a test? Done. Bought your BFF's birthday present? Done. Babysat the neighbor kids for the evening? Done. We don't have to remember those things anymore. But when you tell yourself to "not forget" something, you are wanting to always remember it.

We need this prompting. Otherwise, we can too easily focus only on today, this moment, this worry, this problem, this issue. Yet our memories of what God has already done are just as important (maybe even more so!) and every bit as real. We need some "not forgets" to take up permanent space in our thought closets. These are memories and reminders and images that will never go out of style.

Now is a good time to say to yourself, *Remember the good things God has done.* And then put the rest of your life—the impossible homework, the friend drama, the tension with your mom—on hold and simply think that thought. If you're having trouble focusing, go outside and feel the breeze, breathe in the fresh air, feel the sunlight on your skin, or listen to the rustle of leaves in the wind. And tell yourself again, *Remember the good things God has done.*

Then look around. Try to observe what lies just beyond the surface of your current problem or issue. When you do this, you'll catch a glimpse of the goodness of God. And that's a pretty amazing thing.

Remembering the good things of God sometimes causes you to reflect back on the bad things of life. But don't run away from those painful memories because in those dark, difficult places, we often become more deeply acquainted with the good and comforting presence of God.

## How to Remember

Whenever I'm feeling the need to look back and note God's goodness, I grab a book from a shelf in my thought closet. Actually, I really *do* grab a book—and not just one that exists only in my mind. I do this in a practical way by reviewing some of my journals from the past. I've heard it said that the weakest ink is stronger than the strongest memory. So I write things down.

Journaling is a great way to help yourself look back and remember. You can journal in a regular notebook, in a flowery padded diary, on your computer's hard drive (that's how I do it), or in a blog. The point is to write down your inner thoughts and feelings in a place where you can go back and reread them and apply some practical "not forgets."

We write things down because we're prone to forgetfulness.

In the Old Testament book of Deuteronomy, God urged His people at least eight times to not forget what He had done for them. Sixteen times He told them to remember. His reminders are like Post-it notes stuck on their cabinets, taped to their mirrors, and tucked in their wallets.

The name "Deuteronomy" actually means "second law." It was an obvious reminder, like God's version of a neon sign. God giving His people a neon sign might seem a little silly, but everyone needs reminders. We all need Post-it notes—or sometimes maybe even flashing neon signs—to help us remember things and assign meaning to the memories in our thought closets.

Besides keeping a journal or writing things down, you can do other things so you don't forget what really matters. One thing I have to help me remember things is a ceramic turtle I keep in my jewelry box. *Huh? What does a ceramic turtle have to do with remembering things?* you might be thinking—and I don't blame you! But here's why. Every time I reach for a ring to place on my finger, my hands run across the little turtle. He's there to help me remember things, like the fact that I didn't arrive on this earth all by myself. And the turtle didn't end up in my jewelry box all by itself.

I am *who* I am and *where* I am because of God. That simple reminder keeps me from having an elevated view of myself and helps me to never forget God's work in my life.

Another little reminder I used to carry in my pocket was the worry rock my dad gave me. It was a beautiful stone with a deep thumb-sized impression in its center. My dad used to say it was from him constantly rubbing his thumb on the rock as he worried about me. He gave it to me when I was in my teens as a reminder that I could cast all my worries on God because God cares for me.

I liked to carry that special pebble in my purse or the pocket of my jacket to help ease my nerves. Whenever my hands touched the stone, it helped me remember that God had everything in my life under control and I didn't need to worry.

Think of something you might be able to use to help you remember what really matters. Maybe it's a special photo on the lock screen of your phone. Or some favorite quotes or verses that you've painted on canvases and hung up in your bedroom. Or a photo collage that reminds you of summer camp—the place where you feel closest to God and the place where you met some of your best Christian friends and mentors. These are all fun—and simple—ways to tell yourself to not forget, to look back and remember. And they're important. We all need them. We all need reminders to stop and look at our lives and see what really matters.

## I Will Remember

The psalmist didn't have Post-it notes on his bathroom mirror or an inspirational quote on the lock screen of his phone, but he did have one tool to help him remember. You have the same tool: the ability to choose.

He chose to remember, he disciplined himself to remember, and he willed his soul to remember. This is what he wrote.

> I will remember my song in the night;
> I will meditate with my heart,
> And my spirit ponders...
> I shall remember the deeds of the LORD;
> Surely I will remember Your wonders of old.
> I will meditate on all Your work
> And muse on Your deeds (Psalm 77:6,11-12 NASB).

Did you notice how often he said "I will" or "I shall"? But I didn't share with you the words that preceded all of the "I wills."

Those were words of complaining, wondering, and worrying. Sound familiar? I tend to do that too when I look at my past.

But the psalmist must have remembered the goodness of God in every memory because he switched from complaining to contemplating. It helps us so much when we do the same.

> I have considered the days of old,
> The years of long ago (verse 5).

It's okay to complain for a little bit. But there comes a point—probably sooner than we might think—when we need to move on. Too much complaining isn't healthy for us. It doesn't get us out of the problem zone. It doesn't help us to remain stuck there. So what can we do when we're tempted to keep complaining?

We need to remind ourselves of the good things God has done—and is doing and *will* do—for us. And then we need to meditate on—or spend time thinking deeply about—the works of God.

When you think of meditation, you might think of someone wearing hippie clothes and sitting, legs crossed, in a darkened room saying, "Omm..." But that's not the kind of meditation I'm talking about here!

Meditating is a way of remembering. It is reinforcing what we know. Meditation is an intentional, steady stream of thoughts that run through our thought closets. It's one way we keep our thought closets well stocked with God's promises.

I used to think I had no clue about how to meditate until I realized I unconsciously did it all the time—I worried. Meditating on the past is a form of remembering, but meditating on the future is a form of worry. When I spend time freaking out about a situation or reliving it over and over and over in my mind—even though I know I'm not going to be able to change anything—that's meditating. And that's not a good kind of meditation!

Do you worry and freak out about things that you think might happen? Meditating on things that aren't true—or aren't true yet—can be very unhealthy. It can put you in a really negative place, and that negativity can spread to the people around you.

Negative meditation can also leave your thought closet cluttered with outdated memories that somehow appear to be the latest fashions. This negative kind of self-talk will never be in style, though, and it's nothing you'll ever find useful. It leaves you destined to be clothed with heavy chains rather than enjoying the fashion of freedom. So ask yourself this: *Do I meditate on the things of God, or do I worry about stuff that's out of my control?*

Don't feel bad if you're someone who tends to worry or freak out. You might think it's just your nature and who you are, but with God's help, you can change that. You just need to train your soul to remember and meditate wisely. You must tell yourself to "not forget" all the awesome things God has done for you—and is going to do for you. You also need to spend time meditating on the things of God and His promises.

Look back on all of your scrapbook memories worth keeping—no matter if they make you smile or cry, grin with pride or groan with embarrassment. Take a look in your thought closet to recall the unexpected twists and turns that the road of your life has taken so far—and to wonder about where God might take you in the future. Even though it's hard, remember even the tough stuff—the moments God brought you through—and be grateful for how much you've grown and learned and matured through those experiences.

Remembering can turn even the most difficult memories into stepping-stones on a path of gratitude, contentment, and peace. Whether your most recent experiences have caused you to smile or cry, tuck them away in your thought closet and label them as important reminders of how much God has loved you and provided for you and cared for you along the way.

Even if you don't completely love the way you look or act in those scrapbook pictures, hold on to them. Someday you might not cringe when you look at them, and you might even want to share them with others. You can tell the story of how God was so good to you and how He helped you through a difficult school year or a hard time in your family's history.

So go ahead and give yourself permission to look back. When you do, you gaze into a thought closet that has been fully stocked with the truth of God's faithfulness and goodness, and those times are worth remembering and keeping in a scrapbook.

## *THINGS TO THINK ABOUT*

- What memories have you placed in the scrapbook of your mind? Do they include both the pleasant and the painful?

- What did you learn about yourself from some of the things you remembered?

- Remember, it's important to "not forget." What are the memories and truths you want to (and need to) hold on to?

# PIECE #5
# CHILL

Caroline's phone buzzed with another text message: "Are you ready?"

"For what?" she texted back her friend Mia.

"We're going to the lake, remember?" came Mia's reply.

"Oh no!" Caroline groaned. She had totally forgotten! The weekend had been crazy. Caroline had spent all Saturday at a debate tournament—that had started at seven in the morning—and then had been up past midnight babysitting the neighbor kids. She'd forgotten that the youth group had a service project scheduled early Sunday morning before church. Which meant she'd only gotten about five hours of sleep when her alarm went off that morning.

A Sunday afternoon relaxing with Mia's family on their boat would normally have been great, but Caroline had just remembered the insane amount of homework her English teacher had assigned, all due tomorrow. And that big test in geometry—was that tomorrow or the next day?

All of a sudden, Caroline found herself sobbing. *This is crazy,* she told herself. *I'm usually super busy. This weekend's schedule should be no big deal. Why am I so upset all of a sudden?*

"Hey, Caroline," her dad poked his head into Caroline's room. "You need to clean out the litter box today, remember? You forgot to yesterday."

"Dad! I just can't do one more thing!" Caroline screamed as she continued to sob. What was she going to tell Mia? And how was she ever going to get everything done in a few short hours when she was so completely exhausted?

• • •

Has life ever been going along just fine for you—you're busy, you're happy, you're never bored—but then all of a sudden you reach a breaking point where everything just overwhelms you? Like Caroline, you might realize too late that you had too much stuff on your plate—and you break down sobbing. Or you might not fully understand the reason for your sudden tears, but it usually has a lot to do with exhaustion. When we're stressed out by too much in our lives—school, friendships, church, sports teams, extracurricular activities, dance or band, chores at home, class projects—the result can be raw, unforgiving, relentless tiredness. And this often culminates in a total breakdown and countless tears. Fatigue is no fun.

For Caroline, it wasn't just the five hours of sleep. Or the debate tournament. Or the babysitting. Or the service project. Or the English homework. Or the math test. Or the litter box. Or the lake trip. Or even the fact that a single weekend held all this stuff. For Caroline, it was the buildup of *everything* that caused her to fall apart. Too much stuff—even good stuff—can make you want to just pull the plug on everything, crawl into bed, and sleep, sleep, sleep.

## Meltdown

Sudden meltdowns don't just appear out of nowhere—although they can be helped along by hormones and other factors. Meltdowns usually happen when you're beyond tired physically and emotionally. I like to call it being "soul weary."

One writer states it this way: "Each soul is like a carefully wired circuit breaker that can function splendidly when operating according to its design but which, when overloaded, crackles with the sparks and shorts of a system bearing more than it can hold."

Yep, that's where meltdowns come from! They're most likely to happen when we're overloaded.

At some point, your fatigue is going to become more powerful than your energy. And that usually happens when you don't see it coming. Why don't you see it coming? Because you're so crazy busy that you don't realize you need to chill.

Life is busy. Tons of things demand your time—your friends, your family, your schoolwork, your activities, your chores. Everything seems equally important, and it doesn't seem like we have any time to just do nothing. When you're in a season like this, it seems like so much of your soul talk is revving yourself up: *Come on, one more paper to write! Just a few more volunteer hours to complete! Only two or three more text messages! One more meeting today! Just thirty more minutes of piano practice to log…*

Some girls even resort to using caffeine—drinking iced mochas or caffeinated sodas—to stay awake later so they can get more done, so they can keep going, going, going. But caffeine can make you jittery and affect your sleep…which means you'll be even more tired. Excessive revving up only leads to petering out. And then the tank is empty. Totally dry.

That's why we must tell ourselves *daily* to chill out—and then actually do it!

We set ourselves up for failure when we don't realize we need to rest. You've heard of burnout, haven't you? Researchers define burnout as "a state of physical, emotional, and mental exhaustion caused by long-term involvement in emotionally demanding situations." A lot of people might tell you that these are "the best years of your life." After all, you don't have to worry about a job. Or buying a house. Or taking care of a family. Or any of that other stuff known as "adulting." But make no mistake—teen girls can find themselves in a lot of emotionally demanding situations. Friend drama. Boy stuff. Family conflict. School struggles. Pressure in sports and various activities. Social media issues. The constant comparison of yourself to others. All of those—and there are undoubtedly more—are emotionally demanding situations.

Burnout doesn't occur just because your life has demands that you resent or dread. Even good things you enjoy can be emotionally demanding. And if those emotional demands last a long time without us taking a rest every now and then, burnout is inevitable. When we aren't rested, we burn out, wear out, and even freak out (as Caroline did).

And something else can happen. If we don't tell our souls to chill out every now and then, we are also subject to attack.

## Target

There's a story in the Bible that paints a pretty clear picture of exhaustion and burnout. Do you remember the story of the Israelites making their exodus—their exit journey—from Egypt? Imagine leaving your home on foot and heading out who knows where for who knows how far or how long. The Israelites become totally exhausted—emotionally and physically. God said to Moses, "Remember what the Amalekites did to you along the way when you came out of Egypt. When you were weary and worn out, they met you on your journey and attacked all who were lagging behind" (Deuteronomy 25:17-18).

Who lagged behind? The ones who were feeble, tired, and worn out. The ones who desperately needed to rest.

The enemy didn't go for the strong ones who were setting the pace. Nope, the enemy went after the exhausted, those tired people who were barely hanging on.

Similarly, when we're physically and emotionally spent—when we're completely *done* with everything—we become susceptible to the enemy's attacks. We become easy targets for him, and that's when we melt down. Get sick. Believe lies about ourselves. Scream when we know we shouldn't. Cry uncontrollably. We all-out lose it because of our physical and emotional fatigue.

Rest is crucial, and not only for our tired bodies. Getting eight hours of sleep won't magically make everything about life okay. Our weary souls—our hearts, our minds, our emotions—need rest too. Often, it's easy to recognize when we need more sleep. We find ourselves nodding off in class, yawning nonstop, or drifting off to sleep when we're trying to read. It's more difficult to know when our souls—our hearts, minds, and emotions—require rest.

If you find yourself feeling impatient and snapping at everyone about every little thing, or if you feel like your life is suddenly way too overwhelming, or if you aren't sure why you find yourself crying all the time, you probably need soul rest. Sleeping for eight hours won't provide that. You need to deliberately take time to chill out. You need to do things to calm you down, help you relax, and enable you to draw closer to God, where you can draw on His strength and power and energy.

Clearly, we need to *decide* to rest.

Sometimes we need to tell ourselves, "Okay, you need a break. You're freaking out about absolutely everything, and you need to chill out." We choose to take a break from striving, to quiet the noise of thought, to untangle our knotted feelings. It would be awesome if soul rest automatically happened when the sun went down, wouldn't it? If your homework, your friend drama, your arguments with your siblings—if all that would just magically resolve itself. But that's not how soul rest works. You need to make time to get away from it all.

## Taking Time

One time I was discussing paint samples with a friend. She commented that I was the most colorful blind woman she had ever known. I joked back that I was actually the *only* blind woman she had ever known.

But even so, she's right. For someone who can't see, colors are really important to me. I have vivid memories of the colors I used to see. I remember fondly the delicate pale yellow petals of a buttercup. I loved the many faces of red—warm and cozy splashed on the skin of a tomato or intense and passionate highlighted on a fire engine. As a young teen, I began collecting cobalt-blue Depression glass because I had never seen such a striking shade of blue.

## *Everyone Has a Color*

Because I love color so much—and because I appreciate it so much more now that I can't see it—I choose to see my friends as one of the many hues in my mind's eye. My friend Melinda is the color yellow…soft and tender, warm and inviting. Kathryn, on the other hand, is bright red. She's bounding with energy, passionate, and vivacious. Then there's Karen. She's green—not a dark and hearty hunter green, but somewhere between the soothing shade of an avocado and the warm hue of an artichoke. She's calming, settled, and peaceful.

This might sound silly, but let me explain. Some days I need the color red to invade my life. I need Kathryn's passion to get me going. Other days I'm drawn to the warmth and tenderness of Melinda. And still other days I want to hang out with Karen and let her calm quiet my chaos. What about your friends and family? What color would you assign to each of them—and why? Take a few minutes to write down the colors—and characteristics—of key people in your life. It's kind of fun to do, and it will help you know who to turn to when you need a boost of energy, someone to laugh with, or a calm companion.

List your friends and family members and write their colors beside the names. Have fun with it!

One thing I like to wonder about is, if God were a color, what would it be?

He's more vibrant than a rainbow, more intense than the deepest ocean blue. He's more brilliant than ruby red, more dazzling than amethyst. But I think I see God on most days as green—emerald, jade, sage. He's like a calming, lush, green pasture. To me, God is the color of peace and rest. Maybe that's because God *is* the essence of peace and rest.

When we read about creation in Genesis, we're reminded that each of the six days of creation had a beginning and an end.

> God called the light "day," and the darkness he called "night." And there was evening, and there was morning—the first day (Genesis 1:5).

> God called the vault "sky." And there was evening, and there was morning—the second day (verse 8).

> And there was evening, and there was morning—the third day (verse 13).

> And there was evening, and there was morning—the fourth day (verse 19).

> And there was evening, and there was morning—the fifth day (verse 23).

> God saw all that he had made, and it was very good. And there was evening, and there was morning—the sixth day (verse 31).

As you can see, each of the six days of creation clearly had a beginning and an end, a morning and an evening. But the seventh day—the day God rested—was different. The Bible records no beginning and no end of that day.

> By the seventh day God had finished the work he had been doing; so on the seventh day he rested from all his work. And God blessed the seventh day and made it holy, because on it he rested from all the work of creating that he had done (Genesis 2:2-3).

In other words, God never started resting and He never stopped resting. Ancient scholars believed this was because the nature of God is eternal rest.

Think about that for a minute. Doesn't that just make you

want to paint the walls of your thought closet the color green? God is rest, and He offers His rest to us.

Rest isn't just what God *did* on the seventh day. He didn't take a brief break and then get back to His crazy-busy, overwhelming schedule. Rest is who God *is*.

Rest isn't taking a nap, or deciding we've done enough homework for the night, or choosing to turn off our phone an hour before bedtime. Those can be good choices, but they aren't the kind of rest the Bible is talking about. Real rest means we quiet ourselves before the One who not only gives peace but who is the Prince of Peace. Real rest means we learn to chill out before God and to embrace His calm and His contentment.

When you feel overwhelmed, tell God, "I need Your rest," and He will come to you. It sounds so simple, but it's true. God really will help you turn in your fatigue for faith. Doesn't that sound amazing? It is!

When you're exhausted and irritable, that's the time to turn to God and say, *Hey, eight hours of sleep isn't going to refresh me. I need You to refresh my soul.* And the key isn't just grabbing rest in little bits. You need to take time and settle in to that rest. You— and I!—need to practice *remaining* in God's rest.

Sound impossible? Maybe. Especially when the stressful things in your life—the intense coach, the mountains of homework, the social drama—show no indication of disappearing anytime soon. But remaining in God's rest is totally possible, and the Bible gives us a plan for doing exactly that. Remember King David? He had some *major* stressors in his life, but he was able to turn to God and find rest for his soul. Let's take a look at how he did it.

## The Plan

In Psalm 131, David acknowledged that his soul needed rest. He might have felt zapped emotionally, worn out from pondering, or weary from the demands of leadership. One clue that he needed rest comes from the way he opened his psalm. Evidently faced with information overload and lots of complicated issues, he began by simply pouring out his soul to God.

> Lord, my heart is not proud, nor my eyes haughty;
> Nor do I involve myself in great matters,
> Or in things too difficult for me (Psalm 131:1-2 NASB).

David simply took an honest look at his life and realized that his soul needed rest. We can do the same thing. Right now, take a deep breath and read through this scenario to see if it might be similar to any memory in your own thought closet.

*You grab your stuffed-to-the-brim backpack, sports bag, instrument, and lunch sack. Oh, and that waffle with peanut butter that you didn't quite have time to eat for breakfast. You have hardly enough hands to carry everything! You rush out to your friend's car, hop in, and head for school—music blasting, everyone talking at the same time. You spend the day rushing from class to class, taking tests, trying to figure out why your two best friends aren't talking to each other, and freaking out about the speech you have to give for student council elections. Then it's time for soccer practice, and the coach seems like he's being extra hard on you. After soccer, you and your mom grab dinner at the drive-thru so you can make it to your violin lesson on time. You haven't had much time this week to practice violin—and it shows. Then you head home, where you pop a pod in the Keurig to make yourself a cup of coffee (just for tonight!) so you can stay awake and do homework. But your phone keeps buzzing with text messages from your two best friends who want you to fix their drama. It's hard to juggle doing your math and solving your friends' issues and reading that book for English and…and…and…*

Whew! No wonder you're tired. Moving so quickly from thing to thing. Dealing with all of those people. Trying to accomplish so much. It can make you crazy!

That kind of pace and schedule can create soul insomnia. There's nothing restful about such a filled-to-overflowing life. That's why we, like David, must speak rest to our souls. David's response to his information overload and his complicated issues was to engage in the discipline of rest. He told his soul to put his thoughts, his decisions, and even his feelings on hold for a while and to rest rather than rev! "My soul, find rest in God," he wrote in Psalm 62:5.

Our souls don't find rest in our insane pace or our crazy schedule or our info overload. They ultimately find rest in only God.

But sometimes we're so consumed by the pace we keep that we don't even notice how fast that pace is or how weary our soul has become. We might feel a degree of satisfaction because we've accomplished so much—but that can vanish if we compare ourselves to other girls. How busy we are. How much sleep we got last night. How hard our classes are. How much friend drama we have. How crazy our activity schedule is. But being caught up in our schedules and feeling pleased that we've accomplished so much do not lead to our being truly rested in our souls.

True rest isn't crossing things off the list in your planner. True rest isn't filling up your schedule and then being happy you made it through your day. True rest is only found in God.

## Write Your Own Psalm

When you're feeling like life is crazy-busy, stop. And write a psalm of gratitude to God. I know, it sounds like I'm asking you to add one more thing to your ever-growing to-do list—and I am! But doing this one thing will help you draw closer to God and rest in Him. As you compose your psalm—which doesn't have to be perfect; it simply needs to come from your heart—write down all the ways God has cared for you and protected you.

It might be giving you a loving family and kind friends, helping you through a hard time, or even being born in a free country. Think about it. What has God done to show you He loves you? Take some time to ponder this thought and then list all the ways God has been gracious to you. Be specific.

· · · · · · · · · · · · · · · · · · · · · · · · · · ·

Here's a pretty simple truth: Because God is good, we can rest. I love that. So let's take a nap!

## Yes and No

God gives us rest, but it's up to us to receive it.

> Since the promise of entering his rest still stands, let us be careful that none of you be found to have fallen short of it (Hebrews 4:1).

We need to say *yes* to God's rest. And I'm going to be honest here. To say yes to rest, we have to say no to other things. None of us—especially if we're people pleasers—likes to say no, but chances are if you say yes more than you say no, you need rest.

If you need some help seeing where you need to say no, sit down with your mom or dad or your big sister or your youth group leader. Write down your schedule for a week and see what it looks like. And then together, look for ways you can get more moments to chill and to spend time with God.

And remember, you know yourself pretty well. Other people are going to encourage you to do a lot of things, but ultimately you know how much you can handle. As you get older, you're going to be more and more responsible for setting personal priorities, using your resources wisely, and learning how to make room in your schedule for rest. Now is a great time to be developing those skills.

Bottom line: We need to learn to take care of ourselves—and that includes making sure we get enough rest.

Taking care of yourself doesn't mean you should be selfish and never do anything anyone else asks you to do. But you do need to take care of yourself, so try to find a good balance between worthwhile busyness and life-giving, health-preserving rest.

I've always had trouble saying no because I don't like to let anyone down. But when I say yes too often, I let myself down. And consequently, I let down the people who need me most—like my family and my best friends. *No* is a word that we should easily grab out of our thought closet—with wisdom as our guide.

## Time for Rest

Does it make sense to drive a car with the gas tank on empty? Of course not! But a lot of the time, we keep driving ourselves even though we're on empty. We must discipline ourselves to rest—emotionally, mentally, and physically. So we're going to end this chapter with a few ways we can do that—daily, weekly, and annually.

## Daily Rest

What do you do daily to take care of yourself? Sleep? Eat? Exercise? Take vitamins? It's important to build in daily time to rest mentally, emotionally, and physically. You can do this by reading a chapter of a book just for fun. Or taking a 15-minute power nap. Or going for a walk. Or hanging out in a hammock and drawing. (Coloring books are fun too!) Or taking a long, quiet bubble bath.

Write down some things you will do to build daily rest into your schedule:

## Weekly Rest

You also need time each week to pull back from your busy life. Some weeks you can take a whole day to relax—like if your family is headed out for a hike or going blueberry picking or spending the day at the beach. Other weeks you can only take a few hours to rest.

I've found that I get my best weekly rest when I remove myself from anything that represents work to me. You might need to get away from your house, your study materials, or even your phone. Ride your bike for a few hours. Go to a park, spread out a blanket, and just hang out there. Go to a cute coffeehouse with your best friend and spend time journaling or talking or just being quiet together.

Write down some ways you will build weekly rest into your schedule—and start this week:

### Annual Rest

This type of rest will come into play more when you're a working adult and you're counting down the days until your yearly vacation. In school, you still have annual—or yearly—rests in your life. A big one is summer vacation, a rest from school. Yes! Let's hear it for summer! Your annual rest can also consist of spring break, a family vacation, a week at summer camp, or even a weekend campout. It's important to plan some time each year to abandon your regular routine, your long to-do lists, and your jam-packed life. You might even get really radical and leave your cell phone behind—or at least muzzle it.

Write down some ways you can take advantage of the annual rest that is built into your schedule:

Telling yourself to rest includes telling yourself *how* to rest. So spend some time figuring out what is restful for you. Your definition might be different from your brother's definition or your best friend's definition, and that's okay.

When you feel yourself getting irritated with every little thing, too exhausted to function, and bursting into tears for seemingly no reason at all, you're probably short on rest. That's definitely a time to turn to God for the comfort and rest you can find in His presence. And those are signals that you need to build time into your busy schedule to chill out with Him.

## THINGS TO THINK ABOUT

- What are some warning signs that let you know you might not be getting enough rest? What indicates to you that you're exhausted—physically, emotionally, or mentally?

- What are some things you can do to feel rested?

- In what areas of your life do you need to rest instead of rev?

- Write down a plan for getting more rest in your life—daily, weekly, and annually. Talk about this issue with your parents and come up with a game plan that will help your entire family experience the rest they need in their busy lives.

# 10

*PIECE #6*
# PERSEVERANCE

Natalie felt confident as she strode to the front of the auditorium. She'd spent the past month writing and memorizing a speech for the end-of-the-year assembly, and unlike some of her classmates, Natalie had no trouble speaking in front of large groups. Presentation in front of a class? No problem. Campaign speech for student body president in front of the whole school? Nailed it—and the position. Sure, there were a few more people here today. But she'd written this speech and memorized it. *Owned* it.

The first part of the speech went great. Natalie made eye contact with her audience, paused for dramatic effect at key points, and delivered the witty parts with just the right timing. But then, with about a third of the speech left, something happened. Something major happened. Something that had never, ever happened before happened.

Natalie froze.

And forgot her speech. Entirely.

In that moment, time stood still. The sea of faces in the audience swam in and out of focus. The silence was so *loud*.

A few seconds later, something turned on in Natalie's brain, and she remembered the next word. And the next one. She was able to keep going. But those seconds during which she couldn't recall a thing seemed more like minutes. She tried to end the speech well, to finish as strongly as she'd started. But as she rushed off the stage to the sound of polite applause, she just wanted to find an isolated corner and cry. It didn't matter that she'd finished well. She was completely humiliated—and that dreadful experience would haunt her for a long time. Those moments of silence when her mind was blank were all she could remember. Any positives—the strength of her ideas, the clarity of her delivery—were overshadowed by those seconds of failure.

● ● ●

Life can be rolling along well—everything going your way, no bumps in the road—when all of a sudden you hit a major roadblock. Moments like this can totally take you by surprise—like Natalie's sudden mental blackout—and that sudden failure overwhelms you. You can feel like stepping off the stage and disappearing.

These are the times when you most need to talk to yourself, when you need to tell yourself the positives, when you need to speak truth to your soul and say, *You've got this! You've come so far—don't give up now! You can do it!* Those are times when you need to pull out the perseverance you've put in your thought closet.

## Stepping Out

One school night I found my high schooler, Clayton, despondent and lying on his floor when he was supposed to be finishing a big English project.

"What's going on?" I asked in disbelief. "What about your portfolio? Are you already done?"

He just groaned. "Mom, I'm overwhelmed. This is too much. I'm too tired. There's not enough time. I just can't do it." I bet you've been there too—we all have.

He was paralyzed by his project. It seemed bigger than he was, and instead of forging ahead, he was ready to quit. I sat down on the floor next to him, feeling utterly helpless. No pep talk from Mom would change a thing for him that night. And that's the raw, hard truth. When you're feeling hopeless and like a failure and totally without motivation, you need more than someone else's happy talk. And you need to be more than your own internal cheerleader.

You need to act. You need to do something—anything—to step out of your dilemma. You need to put one foot forward...and then the next. You need a specific, step-by-step plan so you can get going again. Here's what I mean.

### Turn Your Feelings into Actions

If you feel overwhelmed because an essay is due, write the essay. If you feel swamped because a major final is looming, study for the final. If you feel inundated by a horribly messy room, clean the room. Yes, I know that sounds simple. But sometimes the real answers *are* simple. If you have a major project that you're drowning in—even if it's something you haven't even started yet—*do* something. Even if it's a really small something. Get up off the floor. Pick up a pencil. Open up your laptop. Make your bed. Crack open the book and read one page. Don't think too hard about what you're doing. Just *do* it.

Small actions, done steadily, one after another, will slowly shrink the big feeling that is paralyzing you. Remember, all feelings are real, but not all feelings are true. Not all feelings are based on facts. And not all feelings help you to be productive! If the current words in your thought closet run along the lines of *I'll never...* or *There's no way...* or *This is impossible*, stop right there! Actually, *don't* stop. Instead of spending your precious emotional energy lying on the floor thinking negative, unproductive thoughts and whining about how overwhelmed you feel, get up and take action.

Write a to-do list and then do one thing on that list. Just one. Perhaps do what you dread. Tackle the very thing that terrifies you. Let your feelings fuel your action. Make an outline for your essay. Write ten vocab words on index cards to begin studying for your final. Toss all the dirty laundry cluttering your floor into the clothes hamper. What you do doesn't have to be perfect. It just needs to be *done*. And that one action will start the ball rolling and give you the momentum to do the next thing...and the next thing...and the next thing.

## Pass the Pebbles

Someone wisely observed, "Nobody trips over mountains. It is the small pebble that causes you to stumble. Pass all the pebbles in your path, and you will find you have crossed the mountain."

What are some of the pebbles in your path that you need to pass? List a handful. Then write down five or ten things you can do right now to get going and start being productive:

### Affirm Your True Identity

Did you know that who you are and what you struggle with are not the same things? Natalie saw herself as a strong student leader and a confident speaker—until that moment when she drew a blank in front of the whole student body. Her sense of worth crumbled, and she suddenly stopped believing in herself. In that moment, she didn't see the truth, and she started believing a lie. Don't go there! Just because you've failed at something doesn't mean you are a failure. As baseball player Reggie Jackson put it, "Home run hitters strike out a lot." Anyone who succeeds is going to experience some failures in her life.

Consider this example. If you've had a blast at Disneyland or Disney World or adore Disney movies—like *Frozen* or *The Little Mermaid* or *Cinderella*—you'll love this story.

In late 1918, 16-year-old Walt Disney tried to enlist in the military but was turned away because he wasn't old enough to serve. This was just the first of many false starts that he would encounter. Rather than accepting defeat and doing nothing, Disney joined the Red Cross, and for a year he drove an ambulance in France. Unlike most ambulances, which were camouflaged, Walt Disney's was decorated with cartoon characters.

When he returned home from France, he began producing short animated films, but his business didn't work out, and he lost every penny of his savings. But Disney didn't give up. Packing up his unfinished projects, he headed for sunny California, where he and his brother set up shop in their uncle's garage. And they took the next step. The rest is history.

What if 16-year-old Walt had decided he was just too young to do anything useful for his country? What if he hadn't decided to join the Red Cross? What if he'd never started making films? What if he hadn't moved to California?

Put simply, what if he'd quit? No Disney World. No Disneyland. No Mickey Mouse. No Donald Duck. No Disney princesses. Not even one Dalmatian on film! What we would have missed!

The same lesson applies to us. If you quit—if you don't take that next step—the world will lack what you alone can bring to it. And sweet girl, you have no idea what amazing thing that might be! So stop focusing on your mistakes and keep climbing that mountain. Focusing on the mistakes makes us want to give up, but I can guarantee that you've already changed your world for good in more ways than you can imagine. True, big mistakes matter. We need to accept defeat and learn from it. But small triumphs are a really big deal too! So after you stumble or even fall flat on your face, tell yourself the truth—you matter, you can do it, and great things are ahead.

When you're telling yourself the truth, begin with the words *I am*. Keep them front and center in your thought closet. Trust me, you'll want to wear these words for the rest of your life. Remember, *I am* is not the same as *I feel*. Don't let feelings define you; let who you are define your feelings. So go on a major shopping spree and fill your thought closet full of truthful "I ams" based on who God is. I've included a long list of them right here to help your shopping!

## Truth for Your Thought Closet

Here's some truth to tuck away in your thought closet!

I am gifted with power, love, and a sound mind
    (2 Timothy 1:7 NKJV).

I am chosen to make a difference (John 15:16).

I am complete (Colossians 2:9-10).

I am secure in Christ's love (Romans 8:31-39).

I am confident (Philippians 1:6).

I am free from condemnation (Romans 6:16-18; 8:1-2).

I am capable by God's grace and in His strength (Philippians 4:13).

I am spiritually alive (Ephesians 2:5).

I am God's handiwork (Ephesians 2:10).

I am welcome in God's presence (Ephesians 2:18; Hebrews 4:14-16).

I am hidden with Christ in God (Colossians 3:3).

I am valuable to God (1 Corinthians 6:20).

I am a member of God's family (Ephesians 2:19; 1 John 3:1-2).

I am God's treasure (1 Peter 2:9-10).

I am chosen by God (Colossians 3:12).

I am being transformed (2 Corinthians 3:18).

I am a new creation (2 Corinthians 5:17).

I am forgiven (1 John 1:9).

I am an heir of God (Romans 8:17).

I am a friend of God (John 15:15).

. . . . . . . . . . . . . . . . . . . . . . . . . . . . .

What you do and how you feel may seem like the most important things to you. But what really counts is who you are. So figure out your true identity—which is based in Christ—and then act upon it. Don't let your struggles and frustrations define who you are. Instead, use your true identity to properly define your struggles and frustrations—and know that they are not you! If you mess up, try again. If one way doesn't work out, try another. If one path seems wrong, choose a different one. Step by step, pebble by pebble, bit by bit, you'll get through it!

## Speak Truth to Your Soul

A wise penguin in the movie *Happy Feet* declared that "triumph is just trying with a little *oomph!*" I love that. Author Walter Elliott wrote, "Perseverance is not a long race; it is many short races, one after another." Both the wise penguin and the wise author make a good point: What we invest our effort in pays off. Put another way, what you feed grows, and what you starve dies. Think of a plant. If you give it water and sunlight, it grows. But if you put it in a dark room and forget to water it, what happens? It wilts, droops, and eventually dies.

If you continue to feed your feelings of failure and defeat with attention and focus, those dark emotions will grow, invade your thought closet, and take up valuable space in it. If you continue to feed your low self-esteem with *I can't* or *It's too hard for me*, your low self-esteem will grow. But if you begin to starve those thoughts, they will slowly die.

*Okay, that sounds great!* you might be thinking. *But how do I starve those negative thoughts? How do I keep them from taking up space in my thought closet? They're ugly, they don't fit, and I don't want them in there!* You starve them by telling yourself the truth: "I can do all things through [Christ] who strengthens me" (Philippians 4:13 NASB). And use as many statements of truth as it takes! Sometimes you need just a sprinkling, but sometimes you need a major downpour. Keep your Bible—and this book—handy so you can have an easy-to-access supply of truth. A lot of truth.

What ideas and feelings are you feeding? Is it time for you to put those negative thoughts on a major diet and let your damaging self-talk die? Abraham Lincoln once said, "I am a slow walker, but I never walk backward." Keep putting one foot in front of the other. Keep moving forward. With God's help, you can start—and finish—that essay. You can begin studying for—and do well on—that final. You can begin cleaning your room—and be proud of the result when you've completed the task.

### Exercise Discipline

What do you think of when you hear the word "discipline"? Punishment? Strictness? Reprimands and harsh words? Fortunately, I'm talking about a different kind of discipline here. This kind of discipline involves training yourself. It's like getting in shape for basketball or soccer or stretching for ballet or gymnastics. At first, it might be hard. Really hard. But training helps us eventually reach our athletic goals—and training does get easier as we stick with it.

Practicing discipline might not always feel good, but it feeds your self-esteem and makes you productive.

Can I get real with you here? Most of the time when we say *I can't*, we are really saying *I won't*. It's not that we're not able. It's that we're not willing.

Discipline should be tackled one tiny piece at a time, not in big chunks. Remember, one foot in front of the other. Pebble by pebble. Step by step. Small, daily acts of self-discipline can develop a strong, sturdy soul, one protected from the crushing effects of frustration and disappointment and failure.

That's why a girl who speaks truth to herself tells her soul to chill out *and* to press on. Not at the same time, of course! That would be totally confusing. But sometimes rest is more important than revving up. And sometimes pressing on is more important than pulling back.

Let's return to the Israelites and their journey out of Egypt that we explored earlier in this book. When they were cornered by the pursuing Egyptians, the Israelites totally panicked. Instinct probably sent them into "fight or flight" mode—and they were ready to scatter like a flock of birds.

That's when Moses commanded, "Do not be afraid. Stand still, and see the salvation of the LORD" (Exodus 14:13 NKJV). Yet just a couple of verses later, the Lord said, "Tell the Israelites to move on" (Exodus 14:15).

Chill out. And press on. Sometimes you need to stand still, chill out, and wait on God. And sometimes you need to move on, and press on, and follow the path God has for you.

And here's the good news—you don't have to do any of this alone! You can get help from a parent, a friend, a youth leader, a teacher, a mentor…anyone you feel comfortable asking, "Hey, can you help me get going here? Can you show me the next step to take?" Best of all, you have God's Spirit to help guide you. You have full access to His wisdom to help you fill your thought closet with amazing treasures, each of which is a look that is just right for you.

## Keep On

Here's something else that's pretty interesting. We've been talking about filling our thought closets with truthful, encouraging words so that we can easily access them when we're feeling frustrated, feeling like we can't go on. But did you know that it's important to keep that soul talk coming even when things are going well?

We often think that the only time to speak words of perseverance to our souls is when we're on the brink of defeat, at the end of our ropes, or have no clue how to even begin something. True, it's important that you speak words of perseverance then, but those words are also important when your day is going awesome—when you won the student body election, when you got the highest score on the history final, when your debate team took first place.

If we keep telling ourselves to persevere when we're winning, we'll more readily hear that same song when victories are rare.

I can't say it enough: It's important to keep filling our thought closets with words of perseverance so that they're available when we least expect to need them—like right after a major winning streak in our lives. But at that point wouldn't we be the most confident and secure and tuned in to God? Well, something can happen after our steady diet of healthy soul talk and our persevering to victory. We just may set everything aside and bask in the warm glow of sweet success.

We relax. We let down our guard. We dim the light in our thought closets. We become less vigilant about what we're thinking about. And this can put us in danger. As the Bible says, "A little extra sleep, a little more slumber, a little folding of the hands to rest—and poverty will pounce on you like a bandit; scarcity will attack you like an armed robber" (Proverbs 24:33-34 NLT).

Yikes! That's kind of scary. So definitely feed your thought closet with words of strength and encouragement and inspiration when you're unmotivated and feeling like a failure. But keep choosing those same words when things are going well—when you've nailed the essay and completed the huge project and won the race. Keep right on feeding yourself!

## Highs and Lows

There's an interesting story in the Bible that has to do with perseverance and winning. The prophet Elijah was ready to give up—and not because he was defeated, but because he had just won!

Beneath a broom tree in the desert he prayed, "I have had enough, LORD...Take my life" (1 Kings 19:4).

Whoa! That's pretty extreme—especially after his amazing fire-from-heaven victory!

Elijah uttered those weak, pitiful words right after an amazing demonstration of God's power on the peak of Mount Carmel. In response to Elijah's prayer, "the fire of the LORD fell and burned up the sacrifice, the wood, the stones and the soil, and also licked up the water in the trench" (1 Kings 18:38). And Elijah saw his enemies fall to their knees. Then he'd prayed to God to send rain, and the heavens opened up with a thundering deluge (verse 45). Everything was going right for Elijah, yet he'd reached a breaking point—and he had a major meltdown. Elijah went from the height of the mountain to the depths of the valley.

Highs and lows. We all experience both. And sometimes the roller coaster ride makes us just want to quit even when we've been at the height of success. Even when everything—friends, school, activities, church, family—is going awesome. That's because even all that positive energy can leave you drained physically, emotionally, and spiritually. And that feeling of being drained can kill your motivation. We need time to rest after a major winning streak.

So there by the broom tree Elijah was singing the blues. Elijah needed what David had experienced and written about: "He put a new song in my mouth" (Psalm 40:3). That's what all of us need—a fresh, uplifting melody streaming from our thought closets and out into our lives.

## Your Song

Think about music for a minute. *Your* music. What kind of song have you been singing to your soul? What kind of melodies flow from your thought closet when you're feeling discouraged? When you're feeling overwhelmed and overworked and stressed out, what do you sing? When things are going super well and you're on a winning streak, what tune comes from your thought closet? Remember, sometimes you'll be up, and sometimes you'll be down. But your song needs to remain the same. Write down some words to your song here:

. . . . . . . . . . . . . . . . . . . . . . . . . . .

Your thought closet may be full of big-mistake milestones and poorly sung words. You've had—and you will have—times when you just want to quit. During those times, remind yourself to focus on the finish, not on the flaws and the failures. Don't step off the stage before you're finished. Keep pushing through when you forget. Take that first little step—any step—when you have no clue how you're going to get it all done.

Draw words of truth from your thought closet and give yourself a pep talk: *You've got this! You've come so far! Don't give up now! You can do it!* With God's help, you can push through and persevere.

## THINGS TO THINK ABOUT

- When have you gotten stuck in the middle of something or felt like you couldn't even get started? What did you do to get moving? Was it one little step or something big?

- What is the difference between the statements *I am* and *I feel*? What can you do to keep your focus on the *I am* statements?

- When has messing up, forgetting something, or making a mistake made it hard for you to press on and persevere? Maybe you're there now. Before you read the last chapter, take a few minutes and ask God to help you. You can trust Him to help you through anything.

- What song title or lyric can you use in this season of your life when you need to get yourself going? Feel free to make one up!

## 11

## PIECE #7
# HEART

**W**ow, Anna thought. *I knew Madison's house was nice, but I didn't realize it was this nice!*

Anna and Madison had recently met in their homeschool group and totally hit it off. They had practically everything in common—both girls loved dogs, hated broccoli, ran cross-country to train for soccer (but preferred soccer), could not sing *at all*, had one older sister and one younger brother…and the list of similarities just went on and on.

Except for this one thing. Anna lived in a small rented house with her grandma, mom—a single parent—and siblings. Anna and her two siblings shared a room, and their backyard was so tiny you could barely do a cartwheel in it. Madison's house looked like it was straight out of Beverly Hills and had been plopped down in the middle of a giant plantation. Giant swimming pool with hot tub. Chandeliers in practically every room. Three stories. Pasture with horses. Madison's walk-in closet seemed bigger than Anna's entire house!

*Man, if I could live in this house, I would be completely happy. I would never, ever complain. Everything would be perfect!*

• • •

It's easy to think that happiness is simply a matter of habitat—of where we live, what we have, the things around us. We seem to believe that if we could choose our surroundings, our possessions, our circumstances, we would be happy. I'm not so sure.

Anna's story reminds me of a time when my son, Clayton, had his friend Brandon over to visit. Brandon's words caught my attention: "It's hard to make flamingos happy."

*Huh?* I wondered.

"Yeah," consoled Clayton, "I know."

*Flamingos?* I'd just placed a large pizza on the table before my son and his friend. "How do you know the emotional state of a flamingo?" I asked.

Brandon began to explain that with his computer game Zoo Tycoon, he could create natural habitats for animals. He ticked off a quick list of the animals that were easy to satisfy because their habitats weren't very complex.

"Flamingos," Brandon went on, "are never satisfied with their habitats."

"Really?" I asked. "So what kind of habitat do these persnickety birds require?"

The boys went on to talk about the balance between salt water and freshwater. They described the exact amount of sand and savannah grass that flamingos craved.

I sank my teeth into my slice of pizza and thought, *Maybe it's hard to make flamingos happy because they're a lot like people.*

We humans are a persnickety flock too. If life doesn't present just the right balance or if our habitat falls a bit below our standards—like Anna's home did when she compared it to Madison's mansion—we tend to puff out our feathers in indignation. And we become an awful lot like those long-legged, pink-feathered friends of ours.

We start believing that if we could make our habitats—our situations and circumstances and surroundings—perfect, we would be totally happy. But here's the truth: Happiness really has very little to do with our habitat. It has everything to do with our hearts.

## Healthy Heart

The deepest issues of our heart can't be measured in a doctor's office. That's because they're spiritual, not physical. That's because they have to do with our souls, not our bodies.

The healthiest hearts are centered on others, not on ourselves. And a healthy heart is a happy heart.

Helen Keller once wrote, "Many people have a wrong idea of what constitutes true happiness. It is not attained through self-gratification, but through fidelity to a worthy purpose." Knowing that those words came from a woman who, after contracting an illness at 19 months, never saw and never heard, whose habitat was silent and dark, make them incredibly meaningful and worthy of our attention.

When you open the door of your thought closet, what do you see inside? What, for instance, is the main thing on your mind? When you're zoning out, where do your thoughts wander? What is their default? And when you talk to yourself, what are you usually saying?

The purposes that drive your life—the things that you consider most important—*already* fill your thought closet. You can see what they are when you look at your planner, when you look back at your text messages, when you scroll through your social media feed, when you look at the comments your friends have left for you, when you glance at the photo collage in your room.

Chances are, what you're busy with and committed to has a lot to do with *you*—your dreams, your needs, your expectations, your life, your friendships, your activities and hobbies…you, you, you, and you!

Now, there's nothing wrong with posting pictures of your trip to Disneyland or pinning your summer camp photos to a bulletin board. And it's perfectly fine to hang up posters of your favorite athletes or artists and to spend time doing things that make you happy. But too much self-focus, too much concern about our own well-being, will never make us truly happy. In fact, such self-absorption could have the very opposite effect. When we are the center of our universe, sometimes it doesn't take much to ruffle our feathers, and that's when we pout and complain that things aren't perfect for us. Like restless flamingos, we find ourselves quite dissatisfied with our habitat.

## Others

One time at a large arena speaking event, I was heading to lunch. As I looked around for a place to sit, I recognized a cheery voice calling out, "Hey, Jennifer!" It was my friend Pat, already seated with her meal at a table.

"Pat," I said, "you're the first one here. How did you get here so fast?"

With a sassy lilt to her voice, she joked, "Well, I had to hurry to get here before all the selfish people!"

That gave me a good laugh, but it was also a timely reminder. We're often totally aware of other people's selfishness but blind to our own.

As babies, we cry when our needs aren't met. In childhood, we get in trouble for not sharing our toys. And in our teen years, we easily imagine we're the only ones people see when they enter a room. I'm here to tell you that self-centeredness continues on through our adult years. We never totally lose our selfish tendencies.

It's just our human nature to lift ourselves up, to be egocentric. Looking back at my life—and sometimes I don't have to look back far—I can say for sure that the most miserable times of my life have been when I was the most self-centered, self-aware, and self-promoting. When I told myself (and acted as if ), *It's all about me.* I was not a happy girl!

I tell my boys, "Selfish people aren't happy people." And that's a good thing to tell myself too.

When we get the spotlight off our own needs and concerns and problems and instead shine God's love on others, we open the door to having joy in our lives—the true happiness that comes only from God. When we stop obsessing about our own habitat, when we stop trying to make life perfect for ourselves, we can focus on making things better for others. And that's how we truly become happy—when we give to others from our heart.

Becoming a selfless person is a process. It doesn't happen all of a sudden. And it can be a really hard thing to achieve when you're surrounded by peers who like to be in the spotlight. Sure, being the center of attention can seem like fun, but is that what you really want all the time? 24/7? Where does it lead anyway?

When you truly know and appreciate yourself, you don't mind sharing the spotlight with others or even having it turn fully on them. When you know who you are (beloved by God) and you're secure in your identity (a child of the King), selflessness can blossom. And only selfless, other-centered people are truly happy. They've learned this all-important lesson: When we lift others up, we are doing what God created us to do. We are loving others, serving them, and becoming more like Jesus.

And Jesus is the only perfect portrait of selflessness. He demonstrated His other-centeredness in His choice to put our needs ahead of His comfort. He left heaven, lived on this earth, and died on a cross. He was truly selfless, and the apostle Paul instructed us to follow that example.

Do nothing from selfishness or empty conceit, but

with humility of mind regard one another as more
important than yourselves; do not merely look out
for your own personal interests, but also for the
interests of others (Philippians 2:3-4 NASB).

That is the example of Christ, and any flamingo that follows
along that path will be among the happiest birds on the planet.

When we selflessly give of ourselves, we stay connected to
God. Then, as He fills us with His love and compassion for others,
we're able to better connect with people, and that can lead to the
kind of community of support and love God envisioned for us.
Wouldn't you look forward to going to school every day if you
knew that total support and love from everyone you encountered
was waiting for you? No comparisons. No put-downs. No negativity. Just one common goal—learning and growing together.
Jesus's goal was for us all to be one, just as Christ and the Father
are one.

The polar opposite of selflessness is selfishness. You know,
the "It's all about me" attitude. Ironically, self-centeredness like
that actually indicates identity confusion. It's a symptom of not
understanding your true value and purpose, that you were created
by God, are loved by Him, and are called to share His love with
others. When you recognize your secure position in God's uncon-
ditional love and amazing grace, you're able to give attention to
others and shower them with sincere compliments and encouraging words.

So be aware! When you think someone has it all together and
is totally confident, don't let her intimidate you. The truth is,
she really *doesn't* have it all together. What looks like an inflated
opinion is often a flimsy attempt to compensate for the very
opposite, for a complete lack of confidence. Some of the most
outwardly secure people—especially if they act obnoxiously confident and have that "It's all about me" attitude—are actually

super insecure. So instead of getting annoyed with them, try to give them grace instead.

## *Check Yourself*

It's time to give yourself a self-awareness checkup. Take a look at these symptoms. They'll help you know if you're hanging out in the all-about-me section of your thought closet.

- The new girl whose locker is next to yours at school doesn't make eye contact with you. Instead of feeling compassionate for her (she might still be feeling like she doesn't know anyone), you think she's either rude or she doesn't think you're cool enough to talk to.

- Your friend doesn't text you back right away. You think it's because she's busy texting her other friends—and she doesn't like you as much as she likes them. Her not texting back has nothing to do with the fact that she might be busy doing something with her family or she turned her ringer off to study.

- Someone hurrying through the hallway shoves you. Rather than recognizing that all of us are sometimes in a hurry or not paying attention, you sarcastically spout, "What was that? Am I invisible?"

- No one at the youth group party initiates a conversation with you. You expect people to approach you first. The idea of making the initial effort never occurs to you.

- Your mom says, "Somebody left the milk out." You yell, "It wasn't me! You're always blaming me!" You react without even realizing that you were not specifically the target of her comment.

Pay attention to the warning signs of overactive self-awareness. Do you crumble when someone criticizes you? Do you find yourself overly offended by other people's behavior? Do you tend to take every comment you hear personally? If your answer to these questions is yes, you might be prone to think the world revolves around you. And that probably means you aren't fully living out your identity in Christ. (No judgment here! That's a lifelong goal for all of us!)

You're missing out on life when you're focusing on yourself! And, sweet girl, you are way too valuable to live like that.

## Room for Others

You can always make room for others on the shelves of your thought closet. Here are some awesome ways to turn your focus to the people around you.

- Pray that God will take your focus off you and enable you to focus on Him. Ask God to help you do His will. Do you know what God's will for Jesus was? It was to give until it hurt, to become poor so we could become rich, and to die so we could live. God's will for Jesus and His will for us is to be centered on others, to be loving them to the same degree we love ourselves.

- Spend actual time focusing on others—on their

needs, their situations, their desires. These are great things to write about in a journal. Spend time praying for others and actually doing things for others as well.

- Stay connected. Recognize the importance of relationships and being available to others—to your friends, your family, your classmates. Remaining self-centered is easier if you remain isolated. (In other words, flamingos that flock together forget to be so picky about the details of their habitat!)

## True Happiness

When we choose to lift others up, we find that we also are lifted to happier places. If I give someone else a boost, I find that I've climbed higher too. And above all, the Someone we ultimately need to lift up—in the sense of glorify and honor and point people to—is God.

So instead of spending time focusing totally on you—which will only lead to frustration and disappointment—focus on and lift up God. As He grows bigger in your thought closet, you grow smaller. This makes more room for others in your heart as well as your thought closet, and this new, expanded focus will bring you true happiness and joy. But back to the first step of focusing on God. The Bible gives us a great model for doing this: "Praise the LORD, my soul; all my inmost being, praise his holy name" (Psalm 103:1).

We begin to fully enjoy God when, in response to our soul talk, we choose to praise Him. In fact, whenever we fully enjoy God, we can't help but praise Him! When He becomes the focus of our attention, we ourselves no longer fill that spot. And that is key to knowing true happiness.

When we lift up God, we open the door of our thought closets to that warm, steady, beautiful radiance of His presence. When we lift up the Lord, honor His name, and praise Him, it's as if a little bit of heaven rubs off on every part of our day.

> Rejoice in the LORD, O you righteous!
> For praise from the upright is beautiful
> (Psalm 33:1 NKJV).

You might think you have the door to your thought closet locked, bolted, and secured. But you really can't hide what fills those shelves. The pieces in our thought closets color every part of our lives and impact daily conversations. In short, you just can't hide what's in there!

We'll find true happiness—and peace and joy and contentment—when God is the focal point of our thoughts and the One we love with all our heart. As a result, our love—rooted in Him and His love for us—becomes a part of all we think and perceive, all we do and say. And everyone around us will know it!

That's why praising God is not reserved for church only. Praise is an overflow of what's in our thought closets. After all, if you love something, you can't help but talk about it, right?

Praise is part of enjoying anything—music, fashion, sports, flowers, sunsets, books, craft projects, or anything else you might be into. When we enjoy something fully, we can't help but talk about it! The same applies to God. When we enjoy Him fully, we talk about Him.

When we lift up others, we grow smaller. And ultimately, as we lift up God, we find genuine satisfaction in our low position. No, it doesn't make sense to the world. But it makes sense to God. And that should be all that matters.

"As long as you are proud," C.S. Lewis wrote, "you cannot know God. A proud man is always looking down on things and people; and, of course, as long as you are looking down, you cannot see something that is above you."

When we choose to lift God up instead of ourselves, we spend our days looking up instead of down. And we lose ourselves in the wonder of all that He is.

Yes, this is pretty contrary to how our society operates. In fact, it's the opposite of what our culture preaches. We're used to being told to think of ourselves, be our own person, don't let anybody keep us from reaching our goals—and there is a degree of truth to those statements. But it's so much better to lose ourselves and focus on God. There's really no comparison!

The Bible tells us that God takes pleasure in our praise. But there's more going on when we choose to praise Him. When we set aside any worries about our habitats—about what we think will make us happy—and we lose ourselves in the life-shaping, darkness-chasing, happiness-enhancing experience of pure praise of our good and gracious God, we'll truly discover what we were created to do. And we'll experience joy and purpose and all that good stuff that the world can't provide. As you choose to praise God and to do your best to please Him, you become the person He created you to be.

You'll also smile with contentment when you open the door of your thought closet and see it filled with the latest in truth and beauty. And those are the timeless styles that look best on you and always will. Go ahead and put them on! You'll look stunning!

## THINGS TO THINK ABOUT

- Who or what is in the center of your thoughts? If you are the focus of your thoughts, consider what you might need to do to make God and others the focus of your life. What can God do to help? What support and help could His people offer you?

- When you're feeling painfully self-aware, what might you tell yourself about where your attention is focused? What can you do to get the spotlight off of your own needs and concerns and problems?

- After doing some careful soul searching, what purpose are you devoted to? Why? Is it a worthy purpose?

- What steps can you take to place God in the center of your thought closet—and keep Him there? Why does praising Him help you do this?

# AN INVITE

My friend,

I've written a lot about the Bible and Jesus in this book. You may be used to that kind of writing, but if you're not, I want you to experience the relationship that has changed my life.

When I transferred my trust from myself to Christ, that's when I truly saw myself as the person God created me to be. That's when I was able to separate truth from lies. That's also when I finally understood how to talk to myself the way God would talk to me.

God loves you. He created you to know Him and to love Him. But we human beings sin, and our sin separates us from our holy and sinless God. He is perfect, and we're not! So on our own we can't know God intimately or go to heaven to be with Him when we die.

Like God Himself, heaven is also perfect, so only perfection can dwell there. God knew we wouldn't be perfect like Him, yet He loves us and wants us to know Him and be with Him. So if God is perfect and we are imperfect, what can we do about that gap?

Try hard to be good? But how good is good enough?

Volunteer? How do we know if we've volunteered enough?

Go to church? Okay, but how often?

Keep the Ten Commandments? Makes sense, but what happens if I break one?

Here's the truth. Regardless of how good you are, you aren't perfect enough for heaven. Not one of us is. Regardless of how much you volunteer or how often you go to church, you can't earn your way into heaven. There *is* an answer, though. There's a way to God, a remedy for your sin, and a path to heaven: Trust Jesus Christ.

God made a way for you and me to go to heaven. He sent His only Son, Jesus Christ, to die for our sins. When we believe that—when we trust that Jesus is who He said He is and that His death on the cross is enough to pay the consequences of our lifelong sin—then we can live this life in relationship with God and live for eternity in heaven with Him.

So I encourage you to ask God to forgive you for your sins...and then ask Jesus to be your Savior. He will say yes! And you will be aware of His presence in your life as He comes into your life and, among other transforming tasks, helps you sort through your thought closet, tossing the things that don't look good on you and replacing them with the things that are fun, flattering, and fashionable. Replacing less than attractive and unhelpful things with His truth. His grace. His love. His words of encouragement, comfort, and inspiration.

My prayer is that you'll please consider these things. If I am wrong in believing what I am encouraging you to believe, I lose nothing in the long run, for my relationship with Jesus is enabling me to live with purpose and to experience deep satisfaction. And if I am right about my choice to receive God's forgiveness for my sins and to live in relationship with Jesus, I have gained everything, and I want the same for you.

If you want to enter into a relationship with Jesus, you can ask Him to be your Savior and Lord by praying a prayer like this:

*Lord Jesus, I believe You are the Son of God. Thank You for loving me and dying on the cross for my sins. Please forgive me for those sins—and please give me the gift of eternal life. I ask You to be at the center of my life, my heart, and my thought closet. I welcome You to be my Lord and Savior. Your presence in my life will truly give me confidence, purpose, and love to share. So please help me live my life for You and for others.*

*Jennifer*

If you prayed that prayer, please let me know at
www.jenniferrothschild.com.
I can't wait to celebrate with you!

# ALSO BY JENNIFER ROTHSCHILD

## Invisible for Young Women

Jennifer Rothschild knows how easy it is to feel overlooked and invisible. Referring to the Bible's most unusual love story, found in the book of Hosea, Jennifer helps you see that God loves you and cares for you in whatever situation you find yourself in. You will discover that...

- If you wander off, God will find you.
- If you are afraid, He will calm you.
- And even if you give up on Him, He will never give up on you.

No matter where you are, our faithful God sees you and loves you unconditionally. As you read the story of Hosea and Gomer, you'll sense God reaching out to you and saying, "You are mine, and that makes you lovely. You matter to Me; you will never be invisible to Me."

To learn more about Harvest House books and
to read sample chapters, visit our website:

**www.harvesthousepublishers.com**

HARVEST HOUSE PUBLISHERS
EUGENE, OREGON